WELLNESS SPIRITUALITY

WELLNESS
SPIRITUALITY

JOHN J. PILCH ✵

WIPF *&* STOCK · Eugene, Oregon

Wipf and Stock Publishers
199 W 8th Ave, Suite 3
Eugene, OR 97401

Wellness Spirituality
By Pilch, John J.
Copyright©1985 by Pilch, John J.
ISBN 13: 978-1-55635-759-6
Publication date 12/6/2007
Previously published by Crossroad Publishing, 1985

CONTENTS

WELLNESS SPIRITUALITY ✼

INTRODUCTION ✧

A little more than twenty years ago, the Roman Catholic Church convened an ecumenical council that initiated a host of changes in the life of Catholic believers. Yet in a large, Midwestern diocese there remains one priest who has steadfastly resisted initiating any of the approved and legitimate changes until forced into it. In fact it was just last year that he finally yielded and installed a sound system in his Church.

The first Sunday morning that Father Mumbles approached the microphone, he tapped it with his finger three times. Then he said: "Something is wrong with this microphone!" But his patient and long-suffering congregation just automatically responded: "And with you too, Father!"

In the nearly ten years that I have been speaking on the topic of wellness, I have found that all audiences are similar to Father Mumbles's congregation: each member of the audience has his or her own expectations of the speaker or the topic.

For some individuals, wellness relates to nutrition, and the expectation is that the presentation will promote proper diet, whole grain foods, and fish while rejecting red meats and cholesterol. For others, wellness connotes exercise: jogging, aerobic dancing, or swimming. For still others, wellness is a positive outlook on life and involves good mental health.

My understanding of wellness is rather different from the expectations of nearly all my audiences. For me, wellness is not a synonym for good health, physical or mental. You can be terminally ill, mentally retarded, and permanently disabled, yet still have a high level of wellness. On the other hand, you might be an Olympic athletic champion, a gold-medal winner, but use your strength or your beauty to beat your spouse, abuse your children, or be a colossal pain in the neck to all with whom you come into daily contact. Yes, you could be certifiably healthy, but still not be well.

Wellness can be imagined as a line parallel to a health and sickness line. Wellness can coexist with terminal illness as well as with health. Indeed, some of the most well people you might meet are those involved in Make Today Count programs, Live One Day at a Time programs, or Reach to Recovery support groups. Folks in these situations have been touched by a life-threatening disease. That experience has a way of forcing individuals to put their lives in proper perspective, to rearrange priorities, to discover the true meaning of life.

People who have the most difficulty understanding this notion of wellness are often professionals who believe there is only one way of viewing reality: that of their profession. Such individuals claim that sound physical health is the basis for wellness and thereby exclude individuals whose health is incurably deteriorating. Others think "good" mental health is the basis for wellness, and thereby exclude individuals who may not measure up to someone else's yardstick.

More than twenty-five years ago, a physician named Halbert Dunn announced he was retiring from the practice of medicine to embark on a totally new career: wellness! Many recognize him as a founding force in the wellness movement in the United States. His concept of wellness was far broader than physical or mental health.

Today, most people committed to the pursuit of wellness profess such a broad and all-encompassing understanding. Indeed, many insist on a spiritual dimension to wellness, and this is very heartening to a person like myself.

In February, 1981, a made-for-television movie entitled "Pray TV" aired over a major network during prime time. The central character, the Rev. Freddy Stone, portrayed a TV evangelist who reminded the viewing audience that if they had any problems, questions, or concerns, they should call the number shown at the bottom of the television screen: (800) 555–6864. The message and phone number were part of the fictional story.

The telephone company provides such "dummy" phone numbers to legitimate theater groups knowing full well that curious viewers will call the number. Ordinarily in a given three-hour period during which this number is used, the phone company will receive an average of 900 calls. That evening, during "the Rev. Freddy Stone's" appeals, the phone company received 15,000 calls! Even taking into account statistical deviations, the extraordinarily large number of calls suggests a deep spiritual thirst in America, a fact documented by social analysts in their investigations.

In the ten years that I have been pursuing and speaking about wellness, I found the spiritual dimension to be very important. Others share this outlook. But for me this element is so central that I have defined wellness as a holistic spirituality.

Spirituality is quite simply a life-style, a way of living based on an experience of the transcendent, the sacred, God if you will, and shaped in response to that experience. Experience is the key word. The ability to experience life *and* to reflect on that experience to discover its significance and integrate it more consciously into one's personal meaning in life are basic to a wellness-spirituality life-style.

To express this conviction graphically and very directly, I have designed a logo and registered it as the trademark of my approach to wellness. In fact, it appears on the cover of this book. Over the middle "hump" of the letter "W" I have drawn a small, round — bald — head . . . just like mine. Underneath that same hump I have drawn a thin vertical line extending just a bit below the bottom of the letter to represent a human body . . . not quite like mine. With this explanation, a person should be able to see in the redesigned letter "W" a person, standing erect, with arms outstretched. This was the common posture for prayer in antiquity — utilized by pagans, Jews, and Christians. Anyone who sees this redesigned "W" in my spelling of wellness immediately realizes that spirituality, prayer, and such topics will be central to the understanding and discussion.

I also describe this spirituality as "holistic." The former Prime Minister of South Africa, Jan Christiaan Smuts, who first coined this word in his book *Evolution and Holism* (1926), believed that everything in creation was moving together toward the formation of "wholes." Moreover, each "whole" is far greater and much more complex than the sum of all its constituent parts. This is the meaning I attach to the adjective when I use it to describe spirituality. A wellness spirituality that is holistic will produce effects far greater and much more complex than the sum of all the ingredient parts.

For example, the wellness spirituality I have developed includes a strong biblical-Christian foundation with significant

Jewish flavoring and undeniable Polish-ethnic elements. Moreover, the biblical-Christian foundation is decidedly Franciscan as a result of my high-school, college, and theological education and continued free choice. The resulting way of life is far greater and much more complex than the sum of these key ingredients: Christian, Jewish, biblical, Franciscan, and Polish.

A descriptive definition of wellness as a holistic spirituality might sound something like this: wellness is a way of life, a life-style that is based on an experience of God and shaped in response to that experience. This life-style views and lives life as purposeful and pleasurable, seeks out life-sustaining and life-enriching options that are freely and personally chosen at every opportunity. It enhances self-esteem and continually challenges one's values, striving always to sink ever-deeper roots into spiritual values and religious beliefs.

A shorter and handier definition: wellness is one way of making sense out of life. It is not the *only* way of making sense out of life; there are many others, too. For me it is important to make *Christian* sense out of life, though that might not be so important to others. Satisfactorily pursued, wellness ultimately *is* the sense one has made out of life.

In this small book, I propose to explain and reflect on the *Christian* sense I have made out of life by considering the five key elements in my understanding. Wellness entails:

- accepting responsibility for making free choices
- finding personally effective sources of motivation, particularly spiritual values and religious beliefs
- determining one's personal meaning and purpose in life
- identifying life's authentic joys and pleasures
- realizing that change or conversion is a normal part of life

Many people have helped bring the ideas in this book to their present state. To all the laity, religious, and clergy who have participated in my parish missions, retreats, and seminars, I extend sincere gratitude. May they recognize and rightfully rejoice in the gifts they gave me.

YOU ALONE DO IT . . .   ☆ 1

A plastic surgeon in Los Angeles prominently displays a plaque in her waiting room: "At 20 you have the face God gave you; at 60 you have the face you deserve!" It is not intended to lay guilt on her clients so much as it is intended to remind them that each person has—or ought to have—control over his or her personal life.

The person who strives to develop a wellness spirituality must accept responsibility for personal self-determination. In plain English, "you alone do it, but you don't do it alone." An individual pursuing wellness would never say: "The devil made me do it!" or "God made me do it!" Wellness is uniquely and personally designed, personally implemented, personally achieved—or personally "messed up." As Bishop Sheen used to remark: "Each person has to say his own prayers, make his own love, and pay his own taxes." No one can do this to you or for you.

The heart of wellness, therefore, is the ability to make free choices and the willingness to live with the consequences.

Yet even in a country like the United States, where personal freedom is highly prized, few people are really and truly free.

Slices of Life

Remember the television show "Candid Camera"? The staff used to hide a television camera in order to catch people off guard in prearranged and potentially embarrassing situations. The show appears on TV now only irregularly on anniversary occasions. But a psychology professor at Cornell University was so impressed by the show that he asked Alan Funt, its creator, for permission to use some of the skits in a course he taught to undergraduate freshmen on human freedom and authority.

For the first skit, the brawniest young man in class was selected and outfitted with an impressive blue uniform featuring brass buttons and an authoritative-looking badge. He was then sent to a local restaurant where he observed the diners and waited until a patron was served. At that moment, he approached the diner and said: "Excuse me, I'm the food inspector, and I'm here to inspect your meal." He then sat down at the table took the plate from the diner, seasoned it to his liking and proceeded to eat. About one-third of the diners involved in this experiment allowed him to proceed with no questions asked.

In another skit, the class arranged to have a traffic light strung over a sidewalk. It was not near an alley or a street but rather just over a sidewalk. When the light turned red, approximately one-third of the pedestrians stopped in their tracks until the light turned green.

Perhaps the most humorous experiment was the elevator skit. Three students were "planted" on an elevator. When new passengers entered and the doors closed, the three students turned around and faced the rear. In many instances, before the elevator reached the next stop, about one-third of the passengers had done likewise with no questions asked.

The point of the course was to help make students aware of the fact that though human freedom is highly touted in the United States, people are much more prone to conformity than they realize or care to admit.

In the 1980 presidential election, there was a third-party candidate: John Anderson. Wherever I traveled to speak about wellness, the conversation invariably drifted into the elections and the candidates. Sooner or later someone in the group would say something to this effect: "Well, I was going to vote for Anderson, but he doesn't have a chance."

What kind of a consideration is that? In this country we have secret ballots. No one knows for whom another votes. A voter can write her own name on the ballot or vote for his mother. Voting preferably for someone who has a chance rather than for one's freely determined choice is, of course, a free choice though perhaps not as free as it might be.

On election night that year, two hours before the polls closed in California, two of the three major networks projected a winner. It wasn't Anderson. When the word spread to those in California who were still queued up to vote, many turned away and went home. They didn't bother to vote. They didn't care that their votes might add to the winner's landslide or give the losers additional votes. Nor did they care that their votes might make a real difference in closely contested local races. Yes, they made a free choice *not* to vote. The pity is that the projection—like all such projections—was based on predictability, that is, the tendency of human beings to think and act uniformly rather than according to their unique convictions and persuasion.

If that seems like an exaggeration, take this test. Put the book down this minute and go to a bedroom. Yank a pillow out of its pillow case. Chances are there is a tag on the pillow that reads: "Do not remove under penalty of law." When you make the beds and insert the pillow in the pillow case the "wrong way," the tag will stick out and irritate you because you have to restuff the pillow into the case. When you do manage to get the pillow into the case correctly, does that tag sometimes crumple as you try to fall asleep and cause you to wonder why you don't simply cut it off? Has anyone ever knocked at your door and said: "I'm from the Federal Government, and I'm here to examine your pillows?" Newer tags now read: "To be removed only by the purchaser." And pillow-owners obediently snip off the tag.

The central character in *How to Succeed in Business Without Really Trying* was perhaps very representative as he repeated throughout the play/movie: "I do it the company way ... whatever the company says by me is O.K. ... whatever the company thinks I think so too ... wherever the company goes, I'll follow you."

Biblical Traditions

In the traditions of Judaism and Christianity, human freedom is recognized and highly prized. Consider the Genesis story of Adam and Eve. God created a magnificent world for them and a very pleasant garden. Yet in this garden he placed a tree the fruit of which he asked them not to eat. What risky parenting!

If you were invited to an evening meeting and were asked to bake a cake or cookies for the event, would you set them on the kitchen table and ask your family not to touch? If your family is "normal" you can bet some of the cookies will disappear, and if your family is clever, perhaps an inch-thick slice will be removed from the center of the cake with the icing respread so no one will spot the difference. No, the prudent adult will bake the cookies or cake, hide them, and bring home from the meeting for the family to enjoy whatever might be left over.

God is not like that. He set the tree right there in view of his creatures and asked them not to eat of it. Eve mumbled to herself: "You know how nosey I am. Why did you do that? I stick my nose into everything!" And Adam agreed. "If you had to create a tree and ask us not to eat of it, why did you not surround it with vicious guard dogs or a bramble bush?" Eve continued: "The more I look at that fruit, the more I want to eat some." And Adam mused further: "Indeed, not only will we eat the fruit, but when it is gone, we will swing on the branches, strip the tree of its leaves, and if the tree dies, we shall cut it up and use it for firewood. That's what we think of your tree."

I'm paraphrasing, of course. How do you think God reacted to that? Did he say: "Foolish creatures! I'll step in this time and keep you from committing a terrible deed, but you'd better not try that again." Did he play "Father knows best"? Not at all. No, he said: "That doesn't really please me; in fact, it distresses me. But I have not made you my puppets on a string. I have created you with utmost freedom. You can choose to reject me, deny me, insult me — indeed, you can even self-destruct. That's how free I have made you." We moderns use the rather antiseptic word "sin," but the word is fairly accurately represented by the scenario I suggest.

For some who would play a rescuer script or act out of a messiah complex, this is a rather sobering thought. Still, if God so respects human freedom, should humans do less?

Jesus offers a similar lesson. It seems that one day a rich

man approached him and said: "I've kept all the commandments since my youth. I want to be your follower. What should
I do now?" The adults I knew in my youth might have snick-
ered at such a claim. I can hear some of them saying: "Son,
the milk is still wet under your nose. How old are you? Eighteen? Twenty-five? Which commandment are you on: the
third? You haven't lived yet!"

If Jesus thought that, he didn't say it. Instead, he appeared
to be impressed with the rich man's devotion. Taking him at
his word Jesus advised: "If you want to follow me, sell all you
have, give the proceeds to the poor, and come, follow me."
The man responded: "Wait! Let me see if I understand you
correctly. I'm now in the gold market, and though the market
is moving up and down, I got in when gold was selling for thirty-
five dollars an ounce. I'm ahead on this one. And my stock
portfolio is doing nicely, too. E. F. Hutton is my broker, and
when he speaks, more people listen to him than to you, Jesus.
But who's counting? And at work, I'm playing it the 'company way.' If I continue to play my cards right, I should become chief executive officer and perhaps even chairman of
the board. Now you want me to sell the gold, liquidate the
stocks, quit climbing the corporate ladder, give the proceeds
to the poor and come follow you? I'd love to, but I can't. I
won't. I'm sorry."

Jesus did not say, "You dummy! You don't recognize superior wisdom when you hear it!" He simply said: "It will be difficult for that man." Note, he did not say it will be impossible.
And I have a fantasy that when I die and get to heaven, Jesus
and the rich man will be there toasting their feet by the fire-
place (I live in Wisconsin!) and sipping cold Pabst Blue Rib-
bon beer (Milwaukee, Wisconsin!). When he spies me, the
rich man will shout: "Wow, did I make a killing! I got out of
the gold market just before it sank, E. F. Hutton took excel-

lent care of me, and I managed to play the corporate game and retain my integrity. At times it was difficult; some days I thought I wasn't going to make it! But I did, and now I'm here with Jesus and — breaking out into song — 'I did it my way!' How did you get here?" I hope my answer will be "By being the authentic self God intended me to be " rather than "By conforming and doing whatever I was told."

Abuse of Freedom

Some readers might protest that the case is being stacked. People are indeed free and use their free choices routinely and regularly. I agree and offer an example. Have you ever noticed in parking areas what kind of spaces are reserved closest to the store entrances? In my home state these spaces are for the disabled, the handicapped. The symbol is painted in bright yellow on the pavement, a sign is posted featuring the symbol along with a warning that unauthorized parking there could cost as much as a $200 fine. The proper use of this space requires that one display an appropriate license tag indicating the driver is disabled or handicapped. Or if a passenger is disabled, then the international symbol ought to be displayed in the window. And it goes without saying that a disabled person ought to be in the car when it is being used.

Have you ever noticed who parks in such places? At a local pharmacy I am amazed to notice hail and hearty elderly drivers using the spaces. I know of no elderly person who would ever claim that age alone is a disability or handicap, but I have witnessed insensitive elderly persons usurping these spaces often to the disadvantage of a needy person.

On one occasion when I addressed the local chapter of the National Spinal Cord Injury Foundation, one of the wheelchair-bound members sold me a fistfull of bumper stickers. And when I'm not having a particularly fruitful day at the typewriter or in my study, I drive to a large parking lot and watch who parks in the parking spaces designated for the handicapped. When I see an unauthorized use of the space (no disabled person in sight; no special designation on the car) and can verify it to my immediate satisfaction, I remember what Alabama Governor Wallace used to say: "Send 'em a message." I take my bumper sticker and apply it to the car. In stark red letters on a brilliant white background it reads: "I'm inconsiderate; I park in disabled parking places." Then, of course, I drive away because "hell hath no fury like a culprit warned!" The tragedy of this experience is that when we do exercise our human freedom so often it is to the detriment of other human beings.

Fear of Freedom

Still, I believe it is fair to say that, generally speaking, many people are afraid to exercise their human freedom. My wife, Jean, used to be a director of religious education in Catholic parishes. This position is akin to being a principal for the educational enterprise directed to nonparochial students. It is an administrative position involving a high level of involvement with adults and attendance at seemingly endless meetings, especially on weeknights and weekends.

As a home-husband, I'd wait for her to return and try to discover what the situation would call for when she entered the door. Often her step was springy, the mood high, for the meeting went well and much was accomplished. But sometimes her mood was low, her spirit was drooping, and I'd try to cheer her up.

I even discovered what — in general — had discouraged her. A committee would gather and begin to discuss and brainstorm and soon would be traveling in high gear. Then someone would interrupt the process and observe: "We can't do that, it's never been done before!" The entire discussion would collapse and my wife would return home dispirited.

One evening when she came in the door looking discouraged I said, "Jean, while you were gone, I was reading my Hebrew bible." She believed that, so I continued. "It says here that in the beginning, everything was *tohu wabohu* — chaos and void, pitch-black darkness. And God said to himself: Why do I put up with this? Who needs it? I'm God; I can do anything. Perhaps I can create something. Certainly some warmth, to begin with. A sun. That would be nice. A moon, some planets, maybe even some animals and people to keep my mind occupied. The more I think about it, the more I like the idea." And as God was thinking these nice thoughts, out of the pitch-black chaos and void came a voice that said: "That's never been done before."

It made Jean laugh and cheer up a bit, so I decided to continue with my imaginative scripture interpretation. I said: "You know, Jean, there must have come a day in Eve's life when she saw in Adam's eye a glint she never saw there before. She decided that her best bet was to turn and run away from him. As she fled, she looked back over her shoulder and could see Adam in hot pursuit. She must have yelled back to him: "Adam, *that's* never been done before!"

The Risk of Living

Aren't you glad they did it? I am. Otherwise we might not be here. The point of this interpretation is that risk-taking is

central to life. It is even central to the teaching and understanding of Jesus. He told the story about a certain king who
was such a good administrator that he delegated much of his
authority and had a smooth-running kingdom. Everything
was going so well it was boring. So he called his servants together and said: "I'd like to take a trip around the world. I
know I can count on you to keep the homefires burning. I
need some new excitement, so this trip is important to me.
But to put some excitement into your lives as well, I'm going
to entrust to each of you the same amount of money. Trade
with it while I'm gone, and when I return we shall have a set-
tling of accounts."

The king went off and traveled one, two, or three years. He
was having a grand time but began to wonder if he should not
return to his kingdom. Would it still be there? As he approached closer to home he could see his servants off in a distance, and everything looked just as it did when he left. After
he arrived at the palace, he washed and shaved, put on fresh
robes and then went to the meeting hall where he expected
the servants to come and greet him. No sooner had he sat on
the throne when one of the servants came running forward
shouting: "Oh king, oh king, I'm so glad to see you. Boy was I
lucky! You remember the ten pieces of currency you gave each
of us? I lucked out. I got a good tip, I wheeled and I dealed,
and I doubled what you gave me. I now have twenty! Oh king,
I could hardly wait for you to return."

The king was amazed. He thought to himself: "If this continues I shall have really struck it rich. Not only did I have a
successful world tour, but things went even better than I anticipated at home." The king then addressed the servant:
"That's great! I'm delighted with your achievement. You
know, I didn't do too badly on that world tour either. I picked
up many new responsibilities, and in gratitude for what you

have done I shall appoint you over ten of those responsibilities. Well done."

At the edge of the crowd was a grumpy servant who began to complain in a rather loud voice. "Whew, what a show-off! What a big mouth!" The king called him forward and asked: "What's eating you my friend? Come here, tell me what's on your mind."

The servant responded: "Ever since he made that killing that's all we've heard. 'I doubled my money! I doubled my money!' Big deal. We weren't all so lucky. I had a good break, then I had a setback and all I have to show for what you gave me is five additional pieces of currency. I know it's not ten, but it's better than nothing." (He did not realize the irony he had just spoken.)

The king replied: "My friend, you did well. I gave you ten, you earned another five. That makes me five ahead of the game. I'm delighted with your stewardship. Listen, I have many other responsibilities, and I will set you over five of these. In fact, I will see to it that they are not anywhere near the first servant. Then you won't have to listen to the big-mouth anymore."

As the king continued the audience, he spotted one servant who kept ducking behind the others to avoid taking his turn. So the king called him: "My friend, don't be shy. Come forward. Make your accounting, too." The fellow approached the throne and said: "Oh king, when you gave us that currency, I was scared out of my wits. I never had that much money before in my entire life. I'm not adventuresome, and I'm not very clever. I had no idea where to begin, and I was frankly afraid. So I took the money and wrapped it in a napkin for safekeeping. Now that you have returned, I retrieved the money and am returning it to you. Here it is: mint condition, never been used."

The king was furious and commanded that the money be taken from him and given to the first servant. Some American audiences are disturbed when they hear this story and wonder why the man was penalized for using his free choice. Actually, the man was disobedient: he was charged to trade with the currency, and he failed to do that.

But the story is not a story about economics. Jesus teaches nothing about economics. He does, however, teach about life-styles, and that is what this story is about. Jesus contrasts two life-styles. One is "taking a risk." The first two servants in the story took a risk. The other life-style is "playing it safe"; that's what the third servant did. Which life-style does Jesus applaud? Taking a risk!

And why not? Isn't that what he did? He went around the countryside saying: "Herod, you fox! Hanky's your name, and panky's your game! We all know what you're up to with your sister-in-law." Quite true, but speaking about authorities in public in this way simply isn't done, is it? And to his peers, colleagues, the Pharisees, he said: "Phew, you stink! You're rotten to the core! Externally you look nice and fine and religiously observant, but in reality you're like whitewashed graves. Filled with rot and stench!" That's no way to win friends and influence people. Is it any wonder Jesus died in his thirties? The poor man didn't live long enough to have a midlife crisis! Had he kept his mouth shut and played it the company way, he could have retired on a nice pension and enjoyed his Social Security. He chose instead to take a risk.

The practical consequences of these lessons are significant. Here are some illustrations. Not long ago, the *New England Journal of Medicine* published the results of a ten-year study of 3,806 middle-aged men suggesting that lowering blood-cholesterol levels can prevent heart attacks. It quickly became the new version of the anti-cholesterol gospel preached regularly and firmly throughout the land.

At the American College of Cardiology meeting held in San Francisco in 1981, the American Heart Association President, Dr. James Schoenberger, argued emphatically in favor of encouraging the adoption of diets low in saturated fats and cholesterol. But another speaker, Dr. Robert E. Olson of the St. Louis University School of Medicine, countered that while diet does play some role in heart disease, it should not be the centerpiece in the battle against heart attacks.

Both agreed that the known risk factors such as being a man, smoking, obesity, diabetes, hypertension, *and* high blood-cholesterol rates can account for only about *half* the incidence of heart disease.

And then there is the famous "Roseto Story." In the 1950's an Italian community in Roseto, Pennsylvania, which lived a thoroughly Italian life-style replete with many risks to good health was found to have an extraordinarily low incidence of death from coronary heart disease. After an intensive twenty-year study of the community (1955–1975), the investigators concluded that the low prevalence and incidence of coronary heart disease correlated *better* with their ethnic values authentically lived than with the absence or low incidence of any of the accepted risk factors such as cholesterol, smoking, or alcohol consumption.

What then does a wellness perspective propose? Remember the freedom of choice that the Jewish and Christian religious traditions champion. Recall also that just to be alive is to engage in risk. Consider the following items and reflect that each of them is equivalent, that is, each of these elements can increase your chance of death by one-millionth: smoking 1.4 cigarettes, drinking a half-liter of wine, spending 3 hours in a coal mine, living 2 days in New York, or Boston, drinking Miami tap water for one year, eating 40 tablespoons of peanut butter, drinking thirty 12-ounce cans of diet soda.

Similarly, each of these is an equal risk: having 1 chest

x-ray, living 2 months with a cigarette smoker, eating 100 charcoal-broiled steaks.

Risks are unavoidable. The challenge to human beings is to weigh carefully all the options and to select the risk most acceptable in view of the desired outcome. Human beings don't seem to have a good record on first choices. Many second marriages have turned out to be far more successful than the first; many second careers have proven far more satisfying than the first. It may well be that a first choice may cause some people to fall flat on their faces or another part of their anatomy if their weight is differently distributed. But then one must learn to wear with pride the scars of risk and the stretch-marks of revision as one proceeds to explore alternatives.

Some might hesitate and think this is to be nothing more than rationalized selfishness, self-centeredness, or "me-ism" (whatever that means). In reality, it is nothing more than the working out of Jesus' advice to love neighbor as self. He didn't say love neighbor more than oneself or instead of oneself. The self has to be loved first, otherwise there is no measure by which to gauge one's love of neighbor. That is what the text means.

Likewise, Jesus offers the would-be "martyr" (incorrectly understood) a sharp rebuke when he asks: "What does it profit you to save the world, but destroy yourself in the process?" What does it matter to save spouse, children, neighbors, neighborhood, city, state, country, world, cosmos . . . at the expense of one's authentic self? The challenge is almost frightening.

The person who has experienced God and works to shape life in response to that experience may well find that life becomes harder rather than easier. Choices seem weightier and their consequences far-reaching. The risks stand out more starkly than before. If wellness is a spirituality, its personal uniqueness will hinge most crucially on individual acceptance of God's great gift to humankind: freedom of self-determination and the responsibility that accompanies that freedom.

A few years ago when my "native" diocese, Brooklyn, invited me to share my insights with participants in their annual religious-education congress, I visited with my dad, invited him to come with me for the day, and gave him a preview of the message I had prepared. It was in essence the message of this chapter. My dad listened intently, and when I finished I asked his opinion.

He put it this way. "You know our 85-year-old neighbor up the street? Well, he was saying his prayers one night and pointed out to God that he felt the end was approaching. 'Dear God,' he said, 'I've lived a good life. When they said no meat on Fridays, I never had meat on Fridays. Now we can eat meat on Fridays, and I do . . . sometimes. I used to go to Mass on Sunday, never missed. Now we can go on Saturday, and that's good too. I have observed everything I was supposed to observe. And I'll tell you God, life has been *boring!* I can't have much more time to live, but I was thinking that perhaps before I die, I could have some excitement in my life. In fact, the kind of excitement I would like is to win the New York State Lottery. How about it, God? Please.' And he went to sleep. When he checked the lottery results, he hadn't won, so he prayed again to God all the more earnestly and repeated his plea. 'Perhaps you're hard of hearing, God, so let me shout it louder for you. Please put some excitement in my life. Please help me win the lottery!' But when he checked the winners, he was not on the list.

"Finally near exasperation, he pleaded one more time with God. 'Please, God, you know I've been good. You know how dull my life has been. Would it hurt to put a little excitement in my life by allowing me to win the lottery before I die?' When he got settled in bed and began to drift into restful sleep, he suddenly heard a crackling of lighting and a rumble of thunder and then a deep, bass voice that said: '*Buy a Ticket!*'"

My father summed it up superbly: take a risk, buy a ticket, because in shaping your response to the experience of God in your life, "you alone do it."

BUT YOU DON'T DO IT ALONE ✡ 2

The message of chapter 1 is fundamental for my notion of wellness, but by itself it is incomplete. A person could legitimately complain that it is selfish or self-seeking. But when it comes to wellness as a holistic spirituality the complete point is: "You alone do it, but you don't do it alone." The second sentence is as important as the first.

There are at least three obvious notions here. One, in order for a person actually to make and persevere in a decision, no matter how strong the will power, someone in this entire cosmos must believe in him or her. Even if that someone is only "E.T."

Two, while personal freedom is a great gift of God to each individual, there must always be concern for others. Neither I nor my wife smokes tobacco. If you and I are having a meeting and you decide to smoke a cigarette, I am able to tolerate it up to a point—so long as you don't direct the smoke in my face. But if you, I, and my wife are meeting and you feel the need to smoke, we would ask you to refrain or go outside if you can't control that habit. It simply is not worth my wife's subsequent three-day sinus headache from "second-mouth" smoke to let you have a few minutes of pleasure. Concern for the impact of your actions is a give-and-take matter; it involves a sense of mutual responsibility.

Third, even though human personal freedom is something highly cherished in the United States, it is conditioned by roots and tradition. Ethnic heritage, for instance, is a strong influence on the choices one perceives and decides to make. Ethnic outlooks on authority, obedience, and conformity play a large role in the decisions ethnic Americans think they are making quite spontaneously and freely. Further, when one consciously labors at shaping a wellness spirituality, a life-style based on an experience of God and moulded in response to that — perhaps ethnically determined — experience, it is wise to draw upon a congenial spiritual tradition. It is wise to begin with the spiritual tradition into which one was born or reared.

Support

In the 1936 Olympic games, the American Jesse Owens won four gold medals and set eleven track records, the last of which was not broken for forty years! Astounding as this accomplishment was, President Roosevelt did not invite Owens to the White House when he returned from the games. There was no ticker-tape parade to celebrate. Indeed, some doors were closed to him. He became something of a side-show attraction. He raced against horses and later was part of the half-time entertainment at Harlem Globetrotter basketball games.

In 1976, President Gerald Ford invited Owens to the White

House and awarded him the Presidential Medal of Freedom. In 1979, he was diagnosed as having adenocarcinoma, a form of cancer usually associated with heavy cigarette smoking. He died in 1980.

Track is an individualistic sport. While races are run among competitors, a runner actually strives to beat an inner clock. A racer seeks continually to improve a personal record by developing the instrument, the human body, to its highest potential. In many ways, track illustrates the first half of the sentence: "You alone do it."

But the second part of the sentence is equally important: "You don't do it alone!" In Grand Rapids, Michigan, I met a coach who had known Owens personally and said that he smoked so heavily one could detect the nicotine stains clearly on his fingers in spite of the natural color of his skin. There is no way of knowing whether public love, appreciation, and recognition from his fellow countrymen and women might have discouraged the champion from smoking cigarettes at the rate of more than a pack a day for longer than thirty-five years until it contributed to his death. One thing seems clear: there is more to life than physical fitness. Everyone needs human support, confidence, friendship.

Impact

Paul's letters to the Christians at Corinth reflect a troubled relationship. So many aspects of their life-style were deeply disturbing to Paul. Consider some background. Archaeologists excavating Corinth unearthed some thirty-three taverns at the rear of a 100 by 80 foot colonnade. The very name of the city was made into a verb in Greek meaning "to lead a dissolute life," and the phrase "Corinthian girl" was a euphemism for a prostitute. In this light, Paul's concerns in this letter are understandable. The Christians at Corinth seemed to be reverting to old behavior patterns.

But in chapters 8 through 10 there emerges a puzzling discussion about eating meat offered to idols. Considering the grievances mentioned in the first seven chapters, this one sounds tame indeed. Biblical scholar Charles Kennedy in a 1980 report to the Society of Biblical Literature pointed out that the word commonly translated as "meat offered to idols" is better translated as "food offerings to the dead." His on-site investigations of burial places and customs have demonstrated that in antiquity, when people died, they wanted to be buried in small groves alongside the roads leading in and out of the city. On their tombstones they often left an inscription relating how much money they set aside to sponsor regular memorial meals in their honor, which would be eaten right there. Friends would gather there, and passersby were invited to join them. Some tombstones even have holes into which the diners might insert food and drink for the dead. It must also be noted that such meals routinely included "dessert," which in many instances was a sexual orgy.

Paul is therefore concerned *not* with eating meat that has been previously offered to idols, but rather with the meaning and behaviors associated with funeral memorial meals. In 1 Corinthians he quotes their objection: "You say, 'I am free to do as I please' (i.e., all things are lawful)." He then comments, "Of course, I myself believe that, and you may indeed have learned it from me. But I must ask you stop and think: yes, you can do as you please. But is it useful? You can chug-a-lug a quart of gin, but is it useful?"

Then he moves his discussion forward still another step. "Again I quote you: 'I am free to do as I please.' I quite agree and live by that norm myself. But let me ask you to pause and reflect. Is it constructive, edifying, upbuilding? Don't you realize that promiscuity not only gives a bad example but could also lead to herpes?"

Here as in other cases in his letters, Paul insists on the freedom Christians have in Christ to act in accord with conscience. But sensitive pastoral minister that he is, Paul is always concerned about the impact on others. He urges concern for the "weak in faith" (see Romans) or for those who are not of the faith (Corinthians). Such concern is an integral part of the emphasis on accepting responsibility for free self-determination. You might have to temper your freedom in view of the potentially damaging impact it might have on others.

Roots and Tradition

Individual free choices are never really individual. In a certain sense they are communal, for they stem from the influences of many communities in which we have lived or continue to live. Ethnicity is a case in point. Though the United States has long proclaimed itself to be a melting pot, in reality it always was and continues to be a stew pot in which the various ingredients enhance one another without ever surrendering their own unique flavors, textures, and appearances.

I am a second-generation American of Polish descent. I was born in Brooklyn, New York, grew up in a Polish home, and lived in a Polish neighborhood. Indeed, I was bilingual and bicultural before educators began to think of these qualities as valuable! Presently I live in the Midwest, in Milwaukee, Wisconsin, which has a significant German population as well as a strong Polish tradition.

One evening while watching the local news on television, a

commentator of German heritage offered an editorial reflection that went something like this: "My wife and I have two boys. Oh, how we love our sons. When they were growing up, we used to enjoy being with them and playing with them. Now that they are grown, married, and have moved away, we don't see them as frequently, but we do enjoy their visits.

"And I've noticed something. When the boys were young I used to hug them. Now that they're grown, my wife still hugs them, but I don't. How about you men out there? Do you hug your grown sons? Why not? Come on, men, let's not be shy, let's hug our grown sons as we did when they were young."

By this time my anger had reached an exploding point, and I shouted back at the television screen: "Fritz, that's not a 'man' problem, it's a 'Schoenkermann' problem!" Of course, that was not his real name, but I use it to identify his ethnic origins. What the television commentator had done — with all sincerity but insufficient sensitivity — was to turn an ethnic difference into a gender problem.

In my Polish past — and present — adult men regularly hug on greeting one another. So, too, do Italians, Russians, and other ethnic groups. Perhaps hugging is not a common form of greeting between German men. And perhaps it is not a common form of greeting between American men. Still the differences are ethnic and not necessarily gender-linked.

The Slavic penchant for demonstrative affection can sometimes prove embarrassing in the United States, but it could be damaging to attempt to be rid of it. Affection and emotion had enlivened Polish liturgy and piety long before the introduction of the kiss of peace in the liturgy following the Second Vatican Council. One need only read Władysław Reymont's Nobel Prize-winning novel, *The Peasants* to recognize this precious trait.

As I continue to grow older, I realize more and more how

central my Polish ethnicity is to my self-identity and therefore to my wellness. This is not to say that everyone must become Polish. But if spirituality is rooted in an experience of God, that experience is for many Americans conditioned by ethnic traditions. God, Jesus, the Virgin, the saints, and all dimensions of Catholicism are perceived differently by different cultures. To pretend that any one is better or preferable is to detract from the rich pluralism of humankind. My conviction is not any different than Andrew Greeley's devotedness to Celtic spirituality or Joseph Cardinal Bernardin's manifest Italian spirituality.

There is another set of roots or traditions that profoundly influences my wellness spirituality: the Franciscan Christian tradition. My high-school and college education was acquired from Franciscan teachers in Franciscan schools. My philosophical and theological orientations are Franciscan, and my personal choice of spirituality is Franciscan.

In the thirteenth century, two spiritual giants appeared on the world scene: Dominic Guzman and Giovanni di Bernardone, known to posterity as Francis of Assisi. Each was quite different from the other. Dominic was a learned person; Francis called himself illiterate. When followers began to gather around them, each one shaped an "Order." Dominic was interested in preaching and used to carry around in his hip pocket a copy of Matthew's gospel — the one that contains the most "words" of Jesus — with which to evangelize the world. Francis loved the gospels, too, but felt more secure preaching by example than by his words.

Two outstanding early followers of these men were themselves giants: Thomas Aquinas and Bonaventure of Bagnoreggio. They were friends, both were members of the Faculty of Theology at the University of Paris where they taught. One day Thomas brought a manuscript for Bonaventure to review, but there was no response to the knock on his door. Fearing Bonaventure might be ill or, worse yet, dead, Thomas slowly opened the door to peek in. He found Bonaventure with a manuscript open before him but rapt in mystical contemplation. He closed the door and left.

The next day, he told Bonaventure of his visit. The Seraphic Doctor said: "Oh, I was working on a manuscript and at the moment was comparing our two Orders. You know, we both strive for the same goal, but in different ways. For you, the process is 'speculation, then unction,' while for us Franciscans it is 'unction, then speculation.' And oh, that that unction might never cease!"

Bonaventure was talking about the human intellect (speculation) and the human will (unction). The Dominicans affirm the primacy of the intellect and devote themselves above all to speculation intending, of course, that it will lead to contemplation. An exaggerated and distorted example occurred to me in the "real Midwest" (west of the Mississippi River) during one of my journeys when a priest mounted his pulpit and began to lament his parishioners' lack of devotion to the Stations of the Cross. "In Thomistic philosophy," he began, "I learned a long time ago that you can't love something unless you know it. So I'm going to preach on the Stations of the Cross for the next fourteen weeks, and when I'm finished you're gonna love them!" I wasn't there when the series ended, but if things didn't get any better than the first installment of the preaching, the preacher's optimism was misculculated.

The principle, however, is a good one. The Thomistic approach cultivates an intellectual approach to life in the conviction that the clearer one's knowledge and understanding, the easier it will be for a person to make good choices and responsible decisions. The will, after all, is "blind."

The Franciscan approach is just the opposite. Francis was

a romantic, a lover. He and his followers, of whom Bonaventure was one, strongly believed that if a person fell in love first that individual would do everything possible to learn as much as she could about the object of love. If the human will becomes attracted and committed to a person, an ideal, a vision, then it strives to learn all that can be known about that person, ideal, or vision. That knowledge can both increase the love or demonstrate that it is misplaced.

Franciscans, too, know that the human faculty, the will, is "blind," that is, it depends upon the human intellect for its guidance and information. But Franciscans also know that "knowledge is not virtue." If it were, physicians would be the healthiest people in the world, for they know human health in a degree of detail that few others share. Yet physicians are just like many other human beings when it comes to life-style choices. They may know better, but they often prefer not to live according to what they know.

My freely chosen and retained Franciscan heritage with its emphasis upon the primacy of the human will explains — at least in part — why "accepting responsibility for free self-determination" is the cornerstone of my notion of wellness. Keep in mind that it is not a question of accepting one or the other, the intellect or the will. Rather, it is a question of emphasis, of approach, of preference. My socialization as a mainstream United States citizen with its emphasis on human freedom moulds my preference, I'm sure.

And living with the consequences of one's free choices, even the social consequences, is always a challenge. For me, however, the Franciscan tradition is both empowering and liberating. It emboldens its devotee and soothes the pains that often accompany the exercise of such freedom.

Consider a final example. A religious woman, Sister Agnes Mary Mansour, ran for public office in Michigan and was defeated. Sometime later, the governor proposed appointing her to the position of secretary of health and social services, and she determined to leave her then-current position as a college president to accept that appointment. She believed she had all the appropriate permissions.

As events unfolded, it appeared that permissions were either not granted or had been rescinded, and Sister Mansour was faced with an either/or decision: refuse the political appointment or resign from the religious community.

The facts in the case are complex, and few of us are privy to all the data. But good faith seems to characterize all the individuals involved. From that perspective, put yourself into Sister Mansour's place. What would you do? What would you do if someone, perhaps a highly placed and respected authority, said in effect that your experience of God and your response to that experience did not count, were not valid, must be renounced? Would you play it safe or take a risk?

I know what Francis of Assisi did when faced with a similar situation. He always desired to be respectful and obedient to the Lord Pope (as he called him) and to all clergy. Remembering that the clergy of his day were often pitifully ignorant and less than edifying in life-style, one has to be amazed and deeply respectful of Francis's determination.

When shortly after his conversion Francis was joined by as many as twelve followers (including an attorney along with simple folk), Francis wrote a simple rule of favorite gospel passages and journeyed with his companions to Rome to seek the pope's approval, lest they be lumped together with the hordes of similar but heretical groups roaming over Europe at that time.

The pope eyed Francis at a distance in the meeting room. He thought to himself: "Lord, look at him. Everything he's eaten has left traces on that robe. And his followers reek, oh how they stink! What can I do? Since he came here, I don't want to toss him out on his ear. I know what I'll do." So he approached Francis and his "little flock" and commended their courage. The gospel passages they proposed were admirable but perhaps were too difficult or impossible to observe. So he urged them to "play it safe." Why not adopt the Benedictine Rule (now about some 600 years old) or the Augustinian Rule (even older)? That certainly was solid and sound advice.

What did Francis do? Did he hit himself in the head like a medieval "Colombo" and say: "Of course! Why didn't I think of that? That's it. The Benedictine Rule, the Augustinian Rule — time-tested and proven. Who do I think I am trying to write a new and fresh Rule for my followers?" No.

Francis's Italian temper flared, his eyes widened, his body shook. Then he stamped his foot and shouted; "Don't tell me what I should do. The Most High Lord Himself revealed to me that I should live after the manner of the holy gospel; and this I caused to be written down in a few and simple words."

And how did the pope respond? In his *Testament* Francis notes quite simply: "Our Lord the Pope confirmed it for me." Francis of Assisi exemplifies for me the kind of risk-taking enjoined by Jesus and by biblical teaching in general. And though I have imaginatively recreated the experience of Francis, his own words in the *Testament* appended to the Rule are unequivocally clear. "No man showed me what I must do but the Most High Himself..."

Your wellness spirituality need not be Franciscan. But whatever constitutes the cornerstone of your wellness had better be solid and strong. It will have to support a mighty edifice and be able to withstand every kind of attack. Let us proceed now to consider the rest of the edifice that I have built on the Bible and Francis.

MOTIVATION   ☼ 3

M ark Twain is reputed once to have observed: "To give up smoking is easy; I've done it many times." Many people can identify with that sentiment. Nearly everybody would like to know how effectively to "get something started in life, or to keep it going." That is what motivation is concerned with.

In the culture of the United States, sources of motivation have to appeal to individual self-satisfaction and self-fulfillment. Perhaps this is one reason why money is so often used as an incentive. In 1979, an enterprising businessman made his employees an offer they couldn't refuse. One hundred of his employees were overweight and therefore at some risk to their health. If because of this problem they would begin to rely more heavily upon health-care services, the businessman's health insurance costs would likely rise and cut into profits. So he challenged the 100 employees each to lose at least fifteen pounds. If they succeeded, he would pay them twenty-five cents for each pound they lost. Thirteen months later he paid the bounty.

His is not the only such program in the U. S. But one has to wonder about the lasting effect of such money-based motivation. It would be interesting to inquire now more than five years later whether the prizewinners have maintained their reduced weight levels. Have they gone on to lose more weight with no money incentive involved? Or have they relapsed to their previous overweight levels? In other words, what happens when the money is spent or when no money is offered? Isn't it a pity that some individuals can find no more persuasive source of motivation than a monetary reward?

Though there are many books on the market promising to help a person find effective sources of motivation, there seem to be some very basic elements that constitute the rock-bottom elements. Two of these are self-esteem and a clear sense of values.

Self-esteem

A study by the University of Michigan School of Public Health concluded that the people most likely to initiate, maintain, and promote a life-enhancing style of living are those with a high sense of self-esteem. The fact that so many Americans seem to have a rather low sense of self-esteem indicates that this challenge is still quite widespread among us.

The American Cancer Society has developed many of its educational programs with this fact in mind. A series of sound filmstrips designed for elementary-school audiences, grades K through six aims at building self-esteem in order to promote a reasonable chance of having viewers succeed in good resolutions. Some of the episode titles are: "I'm Special," "My Choices," and "My Body." Instead of frightening the viewers with repulsive pictures and facts, they seek to present a positive outlook on life and to show that good living is well within everyone's grasp.

Yet, not everyone has been fortunate enough to receive such positive encouragement early in life. Often the case has been just the opposite. Catholics who were born and educated in the years before the Second Vatican Council, for example, usually received a less than positive orientation toward the human body and human sexuality. Indeed, one of the oft-repeated warnings was that the human body can be (or even actually is) an occasion of sin. A moral theologian, Dr. Daniel Maguire, has jestingly—but accurately—observed that Catholic teaching on sex in that age could be summed up in two sentences: "Sex is dirty. Save it for someone you love."

From the perspective of a later age, it is relatively easy to understand that if this was the actual or perceived teaching, a person could unconsciously decide to smoke out her lungs or pickle up his liver or brain. After all, if the body is an occasion of sin, why protect it, enhance it, develop it? The sooner it can be left behind for greener pastures (i.e., heaven) the better.

Even if this was a common *mis*understanding of Catholic teaching, it was rather widely accepted, often without question. Yet the truth is that Catholic teaching is far different from that understanding. For example, the Franciscan tradition has had a special devotedness to Christ the King. The image is taken from the biblical passion narratives where Jesus was dressed as a king but ironically mocked by the Roman soldiers. The Franciscan tradition, however, is not antiquarian; it does not seek to reinstate something from the past just because it is old. It is not at all interested in establishing royalty and its trappings anywhere in the world.

The technical term for the importance of "Christ the King" in the Franciscan tradition is a belief in "the primacy of Christ."

What this means in plain English is that Christ, the Son of God who became a human being, existed quite clearly in the Father's perspective before any other human being was created. And it was after the pattern of Jesus that all other human beings were shaped. This is how the Franciscans understand the statement in Genesis that God created the first creatures in his image and likeness.

From this perspective, the human body in the Franciscan tradition is shown singular respect. One theologian has even remarked: "If you want to see Jesus, turn around and look at one another. That's the only Jesus you'll see in this life." A Franciscan basis for a wellness spirituality would certainly view pride in one's body as a basic element in self-esteem. No matter how it looks—shapely, rotund, short, tall, proportioned, angular—the human body mirrors in some way the appearance of Jesus. Therefore, the human body deserves respect and care.

A Franciscan wellness spirituality listens carefully to the messages the body sends. Some years ago I conducted a full-day seminar on the healing texts of the New Testament. A reporter from the local daily newspaper attended, and his account of the day was headlined: "Professor Disputes Theory of Miracles." Not one of the other ninety-two people who attended came away with that impression. In fact, two charismatic Catholics were rather shocked at the reporter's article and sent me prophecies for personal consolation.

I was out of town when the article appeared, but at the local parish the ire of some of the parishioners over what they had read was directed at my wife in my absence. She was snubbed and insulted in my stead. Upon my return, I was quite upset but unable to correct anything. A letter of protest to the editor was not printed, and parishioners didn't bother to seek additional information. Perhaps the highlight—if such an

experience can have one—of the entire matter was the archbishop's response to my letter explaining the circumstances of
the newspaper article and hoping it did not cause damage in
the archdiocese. The archbishop said: "If that's all you have
to worry about, don't worry."

I had been traveling extensively around the country at the
time, and that national experience helped me keep the local
experience within proper perspective. But about two months
later when I went for my physical checkup, I explained to my
physician that I was feeling very mild pains in my last finger-
joints. I wasn't worried, but I did want her to be aware of this
new development. She immediately ordered rather extensive
tests for arthritis, all of which came back negative.

What my nonmedical sense told me was that my body was
sending a message. The experience occasioned by the false
report of my presentation on healing had indeed been stressful
to me, but I had managed to handle it well. It didn't prompt a
damaging rise in blood pressure, nor did it occasion a stroke,
heart attack, ulcer, or any other physical effect that severe
stress can induce. Still, the experience was strong, and it did
affect me. I believe the mild pains I had felt in my finger-
joints—and have not felt since—was my body's way of telling
me that the event was powerful and did have a physical effect
on my body. I managed the effects well, and what I felt were
the final results of stress well managed. The body was sending
a message: thanks, and do keep up that vigilance and self-
control. Keeping a strong power base or sense of self-esteem is
a daily task. Some business executives have posted in their of-
fices or on their desks a plaque inscribed with an amusing
pseudo-Latin language proverb: "Non illegitimi carborun-
dum." The English translation is: "Don't let the 'buzzards'
wear you down." Jesus himself warned: "The 'buzzards,' just
like the poor, you will always have with you. Seven times sev-

enty-seven times a day they will try to wear you down, they will plunge in the dagger and twist it around, and think they are doing *me* a favor! Remember, you heard it here first! Don't let them get the better of you."

But how does one maintain self-esteem? Stop believing those lies you have been hearing for such a long time. Consider the following biblical model of a person who has a high sense of self-esteem, but before you do, reflect a while on your answer to two questions. One, how do others perceive you? Two, how do you see yourself? When you are ready, think about the Zacchaeus story (Luke 19:1-10) from the perspective of the same two questions.

How did others see Zacchaeus? For starters, probably with great difficulty: he was short! And short people have never been very popular. Physical anthropologists tell us that we have been growing taller through the centuries. If that seems difficult to appreciate, just recall the historical homes you may have visited in the United States and remember the size of the beds. Two thousand years ago, a person identified as short may well have been no bigger than "E.T."

Zacchaeus was also identified as "rich," and rich people also were never very popular. Yet one must be careful about reading modern notions of rich into the past. In the United States at present there are many millionaires. The present definition of "very rich" includes anyone who has three million or more dollars. Among our ancestors in the faith, these understandings would make no sense. Their view was different and slightly more complex than our understanding. In case of people like Zacchaeus, what identified him as "rich" was that he didn't actually "work" for a living. Didn't work?

What was his job? Tax collector? Not quite; read the text carefully. He was not a tax collector but rather the equivalent of the district supervisor of the I.R.S. In antiquity taxes were levied by Rome, and local citizens bid for the right to collect and transmit them. Zacchaeus won the bid. He then had to hire collectors who would go out and collect the taxes. On top of this tax was added a commission for the collector as well as a commission for the "supervisor." While people have always complained about taxes, there is no record in antiquity of any massive revolt over these taxes.

Well, that makes for three strikes: short, rich, chief of tax collectors. And you know how some people are. The only exercise they ever get is jumping to conclusions, so they concluded that Zacchaeus was a sinner. That, of course, allowed them to hurl verbal and physical insults (rotten vegetables) at him. This, then, is how "others" perceived Zacchaeus.

How did Zacchaeus see himself? What was his own self-image? If nothing else, Zacchaeus had to be courageous. That is not explicitly mentioned in the text, but considering how others viewed him, it must have taken an enormous act of courage just to get up in the morning. Yet he not only gets up and walks out of his home, he even goes to where the crowd gathers and climbs a tree so that he might be able to catch a better glimpse of Jesus.

If Zacchaeus can see Jesus, the crowds can see him. He has either unwittingly or perhaps courageously made himself an even better target for their insults by climbing the tree.

And how does Zacchaeus respond to their murmurs or shouts about his being a sinner? Does he beat his breast and confess his guilt? Hardly. The text says that he "stood his ground." And he then proceeds to explain why he feels secure in this posture. He regularly and routinely gives half of what he owns to the poor. This is not a last-will-and-testament determination; it is a matter of life-style. I have never heard of any millionaire doing that, have you?

He adds: "*If* I have cheated..." He doesn't say that he

cheats for a living. He doesn't say that cheating is an occupational hazard for tax collectors. He uses a conditional clause. It could well happen — perhaps intentionally or perhaps by accident — that he may defraud someone. Then what does he do? Does he deny it? Does he say that the aggrieved party must haul him into a small-claims court or take him to the tax court for settlement? No. If and when he may cheat someone, he gives back fourfold. Fourfold! What did Jewish law say? In Leviticus and Numbers (5) a thief must return everything, plus one-fifth of the value. And in Roman law of the period, only a convicted criminal was required to return fourfold. Zacchaeus goes way beyond both law codes.

But Luke, the story teller, has still more to share. The name Zacchaeus derives from the Hebrew word that means "clean, pure and innocent." Luke has told the story of Mr. Clean, Mr. Pure, and Mr. Innocent, who perhaps even today is not seen in that light but rather is made the butt of unjust epithets like "cheat," "scoundrel," and the like.

And what of Jesus? Jesus is pleased with Zacchaeus. He calls him by his proper identity: son of Abraham, not son of tax collectors. Zacchaeus, like the people of his times, adopted a group identity. And the group he identified with was that devoted to Abraham, not that devoted to tax-collecting. How refreshing to see a biblical personality demonstrate that each individual is bigger and much more than her job. The two are not necessarily connected, especially in the United States. Jesus invites himself to Zacchaeus's home for a bite to eat and offers a pun. "Salvation [Jesus' name in Hebrew means salvaation] has come to this home today." The final sentence is a later addition, for indeed it was Zacchaeus who did the seeking and not Jesus. Jesus simply looked up and there was Zacchaeus, undoubtedly pointed out by the crowd's vocal hostility to him.

Return then to your own "slice of life" that you examined from the perspective of the two earlier questions: "How do others see me?" and "How do I see myself?" In the light of the Zacchaeus story, whose opinion really counts? In the final analysis, self-esteem is a powerful foundation for making truly free choices that stand at the very heart of a wellness life-style and spirituality.

In the first chapter, I referred to the Italian community in Roseto, Pennsylvania, as an example of the benefits of being true to one's ethnicity. During 1955 to 1975, when the study was conducted, about 95 percent of Roseto's total population of 1,650 was Italian. The folks lived thoroughly Italian life-styles. They loved to eat peppers fried in lard along with their pasta. They drank their Chianti with gusto. Prosciutto (Italian ham with a thick rim of fat) was also a favorite. And their choice of exercise was bocce, an Italian lawn-bowling game requiring minimal exertion. Yet, even with this life-style, there was a very low incidence of heart attacks, and until 1970, no one under the age of fifty ever had a heart attack.

This was in rather stark contrast to the rest of the United States, and it prompted a team of researchers headed by Dr. John G. Bruhn, then of the University of Texas Medical Branch, to conduct an intensive study of the population. In the 1964 report, the researchers noted how these people seemed to enjoy life. They were boisterous and unpretentious, a peasant-type society of simple, warm, hospitable people. They exhibited a high degree of mutual trust and were very supportive of one another.

The second ten years of the study noted some marked changes in life-style. Above-ground swimming pools began to appear in backyards, Chevrolets were replaced by Oldsmobiles and Cadillacs, the Italian women even began dieting, and soon the death rate from heart attacks began to increase. The researchers were baffled but concluded that the most significant change that occurred in the second part of the study was that the Italian community gradually "Americanized." Competition replaced trust and cooperation.

The earlier community was marked by stability and predictability. Each person had a clearly defined role. Relationships between men and women were firmly established. The elderly were highly respected and held an important place in their families and in the community. In the second half of the study, these characteristics began to change. The researchers concluded that the low prevalence and incidence of coronary heart disease correlated better with the above characteristics in a society than with the absence of low incidence of any of the conventionally accepted risk factors: cholesterol, smoking, alcohol consumption.

Self-esteem does appear to be one crucial and fundamental element underpinning the ability to make free choices, to be true to oneself, and to establishing the best possible uniquely appropriate wellness life-style.

Clear Values

Some years ago when I used to be senior manpower planner for a health systems agency in the Midwest, I remember reading the results of a study of health professionals conducted by the American Public Health Association. Its conclusion was that health professionals based their life-styles *not* on what they know but upon their values. This insight was driven home to me by my personal physician.

While singing with a professional opera company, I caught a cold that subsequently brought on a nasal infection. My physician correctly diagnosed and treated that problem, but discovered that I also suffered from hypertension. Wisely, she told me: "That is your symptom, and I can manage that. But you must address the underlying problem." I've been grateful ever since that she didn't turn my symptom (the tendency for my blood pressure to elevate) into a problem. And indeed, quitting the frustrating and life-impoverishing job solved the problem, while my physician's medical prescriptions alleviated the symptoms.

Imagine my surprise about three years later when I heard that she herself had suffered a heart attack. My internist, a cardiologist, had a heart attack! Indeed she knows the human heart very well, she understands its needs and its problems — but she would be quick to admit that in her very own life she didn't necessarily live according to all that she knew. She based her life on her values, the chief of which is the practice of medicine, and not necessarily on her wealth of knowledge about the heart and how to take care of it properly.

In truth, the ancient philosophers long ago noted that knowledge is not virtue. Knowing something is no guarantee that the individual will act on that knowledge. Personal values ultimately win the day. That is why it is important to use whatever value-clarification process one chooses to be certain that one's values are consistent.

As a trained biblical scholar, I naturally have an interest in literary forms, both ancient and modern. Indeed, as I travel in this country and in Canada, I collect one such literary form very often: church bulletins. And in my collection I cherish this prize. A Midwestern Catholic congregation published in one of its Sunday bulletins the following announcement: "Monday night, all are invited to meet at the Cathedral for a Pro-Life service. The theme will be 'Gift of Life.'" That kind of announcement is, of course, what one might expect in a church bulletin. In fact, one might wonder whether the announcement might not have appeared at the very top of the page, even ahead of the list of Mass intentions instead of farther down midway through the second column.

Then, just three lines and one announcement later, in this same bulletin, there appears this item: "Tuesday night, Holy Name Society Smoker. Admission, $2.50, free beer, pretzels, popcorn. Proceeds to buy new athletic equipment for eighth-grade teams." Someone should gather the pastoral team together and point out that there is a mixed message on this page: both pro-life and anti-life values receive equal billing. I'm certain they never saw it that way. That is exactly how difficult it is to make certain one's values are clear and consistent.

Conflicts, of course, are inevitable. And encouraging free choices will likely increase conflicts rather than reduce them. Still, it is important to identify the conflicts of values and then devise a suitable strategy for resolving them. Consider the results of a Gallup poll investigating the attitudes of various nations on religious questions. It turns out that Americans believe in the Ten Commandments more than the people of most Western countries, but they hold the Commandments in a prioritized list. Some 93 percent believe thou shalt not kill is valid; only 93 percent think thou shalt not steal is important. Ninety percent accept the commandment to honor father and mother, but only 89 percent agree in not bearing false witness. Not coveting a neighbor's wife is held by 89 percent, while not coveting his property is held by 88 percent. The poor wife just ekes out the goods by a one percent difference. Very last on the list is keep the Sabbath holy; only 57 percent accept that Commandment.

Perhaps the fundamental challenge here is not only for the reader to identify and clarify personal values, but also to realize the priority in which one holds them. If the ranking of the

Ten Commandments in the Gallup poll seems amusing but hardly serious, recall the reactions to Father Andrew Greeley's first novel, *The Cardinal Sins*. Greeley repeated everywhere in the media that he wrote the novel to make a theological point. Christian theology has identified four cardinal sins and has traditionally considered pride to be the worst among them (even worse than lust). He was surprised (yet not surprised) to find that reactions to the two clerical characters in his novel were stronger against the one cleric whose fault was lust than against the other cleric whose fault was ambition, a form of pride. Clarifying values and prioritizing them is a difficult but most necessary task.

A very illuminating article appeared in a 1979 issue of the *Western Journal of Medicine*. The authors reported the story of Reginald Mitchell, a British aeronautics specialist who lived just before the outbreak of the Second world war. In 1933, he discovered that he had cancer. If you realize the progress medicine has made in just fifty years, you can understand that identification of his problem was a greater cause for despair than hope in those days.

In 1934, at the invitation of Hermann Goering, he visited Germany and inspected its air force. He was so impressed by what he saw that he became convinced England needed much better air defenses than it had. Upon his return, he pleaded with government officials until they relented and allowed him to pursue his dream: to complete the construction of a new aircraft that would give England a better chance in air warfare than it might otherwise have.

Mitchell worked from eighteen to twenty hours a day, seven days a week, and his poor health deteriorated even faster. Every physician from whom he sought help in alleviating his pain ordered him to desist from the project and comply with a sound medical regimen. Only one realized such insistence was futile and helped him to see the project to its — and very likely his — end.

On March 5, 1936, Reginald Mitchell was pleased to see the successful test flight of his new aircraft, the British Spitfire. In September, 1936, Mitchell died at the age of forty-two years.

The authors of the article concluded that many people value things that enhance the meaning and quality of their lives *much more* than they value health itself. Many people often engage in health-threatening risks because they enhance the meaning and quality of life. The authors concede that the choices of individual purpose and direction in life are unquestionably the domain of each person. Health professionals must realize that as much as they know and can offer to humankind from the perspective of the scientific practice of medicine, the quality and meaning of life will be found in a much broader perspective than that. In other words, what do humans claim to be the greatest of all values, health or life? Qoheleth offered his answer when the sage said he'd rather be a live pussycat than a dead lion.

Why Bother?

The ability and courage to make good choices has to rest solidly on a keen sense of personal self-esteem, a realistic self-image, as well as on a continually reassessed and refined set of values. As the examples in this chapter indicated, that might sound nice, but it is very difficult and often painful to put into practice in one's personal life. So why bother? Why not just do it the company way?

The answer — for believers, at any rate — is found stated rather boldly in the Jewish scriptures. At least three times in

Leviticus we read words to this effect: "Since I, the Lord, brought you up from the land of Egypt that I might be your God, you shall be holy, because I am holy" (11:45; see also 19:2 and 20:26). God himself is thus the basic source of Jewish motivation for pursuing a wellness spirituality. Becoming holy is the appropriate way to shape one's life in response to the exodus experience.

But what does that mean, concretely? Jesus interpreted it for his followers, and the evangelists presented that with their own nuances. Matthew (5:48) reports Jesus urging his disciples to be perfect as the Father is perfect. This is how their righteousness will surpass that of the scribes and the Pharisees (5:20). Matthew has turned to Deuteronomy 18:13 for his inspiration: "You, however, must be altogether wholehearted in the service of the Lord your God." The Hebrew word for wholehearted means complete, entire, integral, that is, exhibiting a single-minded concern to do God's will. To be perfect as the Father is perfect is to desire the perfect fulfillment of the divine will. In John's gospel that means that believers should have "life, and have it to the full."

Luke reports it somewhat differently. He claims Jesus would have us be compassionate as the Father is compassionate (6:36). The Hebrew word behind the Greek translation derives from the word that also means womb. Some would say that Luke's Jesus would want his followers to adopt the feminine aspect of God, the gentle and compassionate dimension. True as that might be, there may also be yet another viewpoint. In the Hebrew scriptures, the word compassionate often describes God but very rarely human beings. Luke's Jesus — just like the author of Leviticus — wants us to be nothing less than Godlike.

This can be frightening. But Paul makes it easier. "Imitate me" he says, "as I imitate Christ" (1 Corinthians 11:1; see also 1 Thessalonians 1:5; Philemon 3:17). Moderns would call that *chutzpah*. How could anyone dare to be so bold? Paul's is certainly not the only way to imitate Christ, or to be perfect, compassionate, holy as the Father is holy. Quite true. And yet the biblical challenge is clear, directed to all without distinction and inflexible. Anyone who conscientiously strives to meet it should have no difficulty saying confidently with Paul: "Imitate me!" This is certainly not the only way of doing it, but it is a trustworthy and reliable way. And that is the uniqueness which characterizes the wellness, holistic spirituality. It is pursued because God wills it. And when it is achieved and expressed in a personal uniqueness, it is not only worthy of admiration but also deserving of imitation.

PURPOSE IN LIFE ✡ 4

I t did not dawn on me then, but when I was young
I had learned all about the true purpose and meaning
in life from my old *Baltimore Catechism*, in Polish. "Dlaczego
Pan Bog cie stworzył?" was one of the very first questions.
"Why did God make you"? The answer: "God made me to
know him, love him, and serve him faithfully here on earth,
and then to be happy with him forever in heaven."

But in reality, we all learned the purpose and meaning of
life not from the catechism, but from our English readers.
(My Polish reader was constructed in a rather different and
interesting way.) My English reader in 1942 featured the
"typical American Family": Mother, Father, Dick, Jane,
Spot and Fluff. In my reader, I watched Dick and Father
play baseball together, wash the car, and go fishing. But
Mother and Jane dusted around the house, went shopping,
and baked cookies together. And Jane made me very angry.
She was doing my "jobs"! As the oldest of three boys in a
family with no girls, I learned how to clean the house, do the

laundry, cook the meals, mend socks, and a host of other things my sister might have learned had I had one.

The reader we used may have accomplished its goal to help youngsters learn the basic skills of literacy in the English language. But it also accomplished something else: it socialized youngsters into the proper, sterotypically sex-linked social roles in American society. But fortunately, the situation has begun to change in most dramatic ways.

Anyone who lived in Austin, Texas, in recent years may have answered the doorbell only to be met by an interesting surprise. There stood Bill Barnes, who smiled widely and said: "Hi! My name is Bill Barnes, and I'm probably the only bearded Avon Lady in town!" Indeed, Bill was one of 20,000 Avon gentlemen, who constitute approximately 5 percent of the total Avon sales force.

How did this happen? Bill came home from work one day and said: "I've had it up to here with that job. That retired military colonel who is the executive reminds me every day of the contradiction in terms expressed by the phrase: 'military intelligence'! Now, I can continue working there and bringing home an excellent salary and fringe benefits, but at this rate I will die early, make a handsome corpse, and leave you a wealthy widow. Or I can quit that job, and we can adjust our style of living. And maybe I'll be able to spend many more years together with you and the family."

His wife looked at him and said: "Do you think sitting home is fun? Do you think bringing up our three young children is a picnic? You know what Plato said: 'Children are the most difficult of all beasts to manage.' Why don't I find a job outside the home for a good salary, and you stay here and take care of the children and house affairs?"

Before she could continue, Bill grabbed her hand, shook it firmly and said: "It's a deal!" And she did find an excellent job outside the home that enabled her to take good financial care of the family, while Bill stayed home, took care of the children, and wrote poetry . . . which is what he really wanted to do with his life.

And now that the children are older, Bill has time for a part-time job outside the home and can still be home when they return from school. The situation is not only humorous, but true and repeating itself with increasing frequency in this country.

This anecdote suggests two topics for consideration as part of a personally determined meaning and purpose in life: one's occupation or ministry, one's vocation or state in life.

Forming an Occupation or Ministry

Even though the popular proverb claims that "A person was made to work, like the bird was made to fly," no one would seriously admit that "work" is *the* total purpose and meaning of life. It may form part of the total purpose, but it is not in itself what life is all about. Still, work plays such a large part in the lives of Americans that Gabriel Moran is quite correct when he says that if religious education does not talk about work, then it is a failure, since work is where the majority of people spend most of their lives.

It was Qoheleth (also know as Ecclesiastes) who explored the meaning and purpose of life in the Jewish scriptures. In his mature years, he gathered up his reflections and said (in imitation of Doctor Doolittle): 'I've been around, I've seen the world, I can tell you stories that would quite astound you. I've been to school, I'm no fool, I've been from Liverpool to Istanbul. . . . I tried everything there is to try, done everything there is to do, and my conclusion is: 'It's all a crock!' "

He quite anticipated his audience's half-skeptical and half-supportive laughter, so he continued: "I knew you'd laugh. Well, I'll give you three examples from my life experience. See if I lie. Let's consider pleasure, learning, and work.

"When I was young, I thought pleasure was the chief meaning and purpose of life. So I ate every food I was offered, drank everything in sight, went to parties, played games. You know what I discovered? I discovered there is a very narrow line between pleasure and pain. When you chug-a-lug enough beer over the weekend, soon the men with the small hammers are at work in your skull, a cotton-in-the-mouth feeling possesses you, and you wonder why you did it. When, like me, you've worshiped enough at the 'porcelain altar' you realize that excesses in pleasure cannot be the meaning and purpose of life.

"By this time, I'm in my thirties, and I decide it's time to 'get smart.' So I enroll in school. I go to day school, night school, summer school. I take workshops and seminars. I pursue degrees and certificates. You know what I gradually discover? It's not *what* you know, but *whom* you know that counts more than anything else. So why am I studying and pursuing knowledge? In a nation that applauds anti-intellectualism and penalizes college education and graduate degrees, why am I wasting my time? This can't be the meaning and purpose in life.

"By now, I'm entering my midlife crisis. I haven't held a serious job yet. So I determine to enter the work force. I work a daytime job. Then I need more money, so I take a nighttime job. I work overtime, time-and-a-half, double-time. I work my fingers to the bone. Then one night on the job, my partner keels over, dead, from excessive work. I say to myself: 'Wow, the poor fool worked himself to death!' But before his corpse was cold, his heirs had spent their entire inheritance. And I asked myself: Why am I working so hard?"

This is, of course, a paraphrase and interpretation of Qoheleth. But the scripture can be relevant if appropriately focused on contemporary life, and Qoheleth raises some very demanding questions.

Throughout his reflections he keeps repeating like a refrain: "So eat, drink, be merry, enjoy the wife of your youth." Many people consider this hedonistic or pessimistic. But in a sense, it's what Bill Barnes determined to do in his own life, isn't it?

And Qoheleth's conclusion is actually found—like most conclusions—at the end of his book. There he says: "When all is said and done, listen to the words of this veteran of life. The entire meaning and purpose of life is: love God, keep his Commandments, and have a ball!"

Jesus, too, offers some reflections on work as part of the overall meaning in life. One day he was addressing a crowd and told the story of a man who had a bumper crop. It was so huge it wouldn't fit into his barns. So he determined to tear down the barns, build larger ones, and establish his "I.R.A. account for life." That night the Lord God said to him: "Poor fool, now you must die! What good is your I.R.A. account now?"

The people in the audience were a little puzzled. Was Jesus discouraging tne virtues of industriousness, prudent care for the future? Was he encouraging laziness, destruction of excessive produce? Jesus explained. Without pointing a finger, but selecting a masculine Aramaic noun, he addressed the men: "Look at the birds of the air. They don't plow, sow, till, or reap. And yet I never saw a bird die of malnutrition, did you?"

The men were angry. Steam was shooting out of their ears. It sounded as if Jesus were undermining the economic system itself. But the women were smiling, for Jesus had finally "stuck

it to" these workaholic men. Maybe now they'd be more at-
tentive to other matters. Then once again refusing to point
fingers, but making it nevertheless clear whom he was addressing, Jesus selected a feminine Aramaic noun. "Look at
the anemones, the 'lilies of the field.' See how pretty and deli-
cate they are? There isn't a woman here whose entire closet
full of togas can match them in beauty. Yet they are here
today and dried up tomorrow. We burn them in the earth-
oven." And now the women were upset. Jesus had effectively
snapped their garters.

To bring the entire discussion to a conclusion Jesus advised
the entire audience: "Don't worry about what you're going to
eat, or wear. If God takes care of birds and flowers, won't he
take care of you even more? No, seek first the reign of God
and his righteousness, and everything else will be given to
you."

These are difficult lessons for modern men and women to
grasp: to love God, keep his Commandments, and enjoy life
or to seek above all the reign of God, and everything else one
considers important will come as well. Indeed, a sixteen-year
study of 350,000 workers from 7,000 corporations discovered
that four out of five of them were misemployed and would be
happier elsewhere. People would rather work and be miser-
able than change jobs for a lesser-paying position, or take
some time off from work to consider more satisfying life-
situations.

John the Evangelist offers an interesting insight on what
work might really mean in human life. In 14:12, Jesus says: "I
solemnly assure you, the one who has faith in me will do the
works I do and greater far than these." That is a powerful
promise. Is anyone doing that today?

The Greek word that John's Jesus uses here to describe what
he does is used only by Jesus and only to describe what he does

in this gospel. That word, *erga*, was used by the Greek trans-
lators of the Jewish scriptures to describe what God does. And
God's two great works praised and celebrated throughout the
Jewish scriptures are creation and redemption. The English
translation of these theological jargon words makes the ideas
a little clearer: in creation, God bestowed life; in redemption, he restored meaning to life. By redeeming the Israelites
from bondage and forced labor in Egypt, God did not abolish
work but rather restored human meaning and purpose to this
activity.

By placing this same Greek word on Jesus' lips, the implica-
tion is that Jesus' work is also one of creation and redemption,
of giving life and restoring meaning to life. Surely, when he
raised Lazarus and fed the multitudes, Jesus engaged in a life-
giving activity. And when he restored sight to the man born
blind, healed the paralytic by the pool, changed water into
wine at Cana for the wedding feast, he was restoring meaning
to life, enriching the meaning of life.

In this perspective, Jesus' promise becomes an examination
of conscience for a believer. Is the work you do life-giving?
Does it enhance the meaning and purpose of life, or deprive
life of hope, meaning, purposefulness? When I was a young-
ster, my father used to work for a manufacturer of munitions
during World War II. Like all Americans in that era, he was
proud of his work and the contribution it made to the war
effort. I recall that when my mother was in the hospital giving
birth to my youngest brother, my father brought home some
"dead" (i.e., not loaded) shells and fastened a variety of sizes
to the cannister cans as "handles." My mother was a little
nervous upon returning from the hospital to see those bullets
standing tall atop her cannisters, but when she realized the
ammunition was not live, she too shared in my father's pride
in workmanship.

Today we live in a different age, a different climate, and we too have different attitudes. Today a bishop such as Leroy Matthiessen of Amarillo, Texas has asked the people of his diocese to reflect upon their own jobs if they should be in the area of arms production. Bishop Matthiessen would propose the test of John's gospel: does your work, your product give life or take it away? Does your work add to the enrichment of life's meaning or suggest that life has no meaning or purpose? These are difficult reflections, and the bishops—while voicing personal opinion and choices—impose no such opinion or choices on others.

This is quite in line with the notion of wellness as a holistic spirituality developed within these pages. An individual constructing a wellness spirituality that responds to a unique and personal experience of God will have to determine for herself or himself whether participation or refusal to participate in the production of nuclear weapons fits well or ill with that experience. The text from John and its context within his gospel, as well as within the entire Bible, offers just one point for reflection. There are countless others, but reflect one must.

The Benedictines, who recently celebrated the sesquimillenial (1,500th) anniversary of their existence, have been famous for their motto: work and pray. They are experts on the place of work in the totality of human experience. The Conference of American Benedictine Prioresses published a series of brief reflections on the proper adaption of their ancient ideals to contemporary circumstances, and in a 1980 statement entitled "Of All Good Gifts" they wrote: "In Benedictine communities, the purpose of work is not unlimited productivity and profits, but providing services for others, opportunity for personal development, and a simple mode of life." The richness of the reflections in the Prioresses' statement made it quite clear that Benedictine wellness is solidly rooted in tradition but keenly sensitive to the special needs of this—and every—culture, as well as to the uniqueness of individuals who strive to live the Benedictine tradition. It is a stimulating example of the kind of reflection I am proposing in this chapter. The Benedictine experience of balancing work and prayer, labor and leisure deserves a wider exposure than it has received in the past. Our time and culture stand in real need of this witness from a rich Christian tradition.

Clink Thomson's biblically rooted fable (see Luke 12:15-21) of the Ant and the Grasshopper is a fitting conclusion to this reflection on the place of work in human life. "Once upon a time, an ant and a grasshopper lived in the same village. The ant was very industrious and, through hard work, acquired himself a theology degree and a large congregation. He was very farsighted and spent the whole summer building up the parish larder—so he and his congregation could enjoy the harsh winter.

"The grasshopper was very lazy and spent his summer nights in honky-tonks—eating, drinking, and making merry. He was a good musician, though, and earned enough playing for pennies in the park to pay for his daily bar tab.

"When winter came and no one came to the park, the prodigal grasshopper went to the parsonage and asked the ant for a few grains of wheat.

"You spent your summer fiddling around, and now you expect my hard-working congregation to feed you," chided the ant, ever the good steward.

"I'll be happy to play for your congregation," offered the grasshopper, thinking fast.

"I need someone to keep the books," said the wise ant.

"I need someone to teach scripture," said the ant.

"I can play Bach," said the grasshopper.

"I need a social worker," said the caring ant.

"I can make people dance," said the grasshopper.

"In church?" asked the Rev. Ant. "Here, you take this hand-out and go in peace."

"The grasshopper left with a few grains of wheat and a heavy heart. That night the ant choked and died on a piece of meat — without ever hearing any good music."

Forming a Vocation or State in Life

Anyone who watches the day or nighttime television soap operas sooner or later must ask the question: is this drama reflecting life? If it is, then we are to be pitied. Or is this drama shaping life? If it is, then we ought to be angry. It would seem as if no character in the soap operas is capable of having more than one close friend of the opposite sex at one time. The endless round of musical friendships or musical marriages has to give one pause.

Pastoral experience in the Roman Catholic communion over the last quarter-century has prompted a certain change in approach to the human task of deciding whether or not to get married, as well as to the length of time needed to make that decision. I recall from my youth that the prevalent advice was to date for six months. Anything longer than that without a decision to marry could become "an occasion of sin." That outlook has mercifully changed, and in the State of Wisconsin where I presently live, all the five dioceses have adopted a common policy toward the sacrament of matrimony. The general advice to those who decide on marriage is to allow at least an additional four to six months for the completion of the process involved in this policy.

The change is a welcome one in the light of our improved understanding of how human beings grow and develop. Since life expectancy has dramatically increased since the turn of this century, marriages now last much longer than they used to. For this reason, they need not be entered into quite so early, and those who do decide to marry need a different preparation than was needed in the past.

The life-stages researcher Daniel Levinson discovered that at this time in history, a critical prerequisite for successful marriage is the developed capability of having "adult peer relationships" with others, especially with members of the opposite sex. Levinson worked exclusively with forty men, and so his comments are especially relevant to men. The kind of relationship he has in mind involves a wide variety of components in many different combinations: admiration, respect, dependency, sexuality, affection, emotional intimacy, and many, many others.

His research revealed that preadult development never prepared men sufficiently to pursue these challenges, and therefore most men in their twenties are not really capable of making a lasting commitment to wife and family, nor are they really capable of a "highly loving, sexually free and emotionally intimate relationship." Many men still marry within a stereotypical framework quite often linked with the male's occupation.

This dimension of a wellness spirituality is not only related to one's self-image and self-esteem, but is also a very important segment of one's purpose and meaning in life. Since sexual stereotypes continue to abound and shape personal meaning and direction in life, it is critical to consider them in this connection.

Even celibate religious communities realize how fundamental this is to personal fulfillment and wholeness. The Maryknoll psychiatrist, Sister Maria Rieckelmann, wrote the following sentiments in a dedicatory introduction to a new magazine entitled, *Human Development* "[These are] times that call us to true friendships as persons in far more integrated communities of 'women and men' who are capable of breaking out of the rigid categories of clerical/lay, religious/secular, male/female." This is a powerful challenge to all.

The 1983 Constitutions of the Sisters of the Blessed Virgin Mary (Dubuque, Iowa) pointedly note: "Through consecrated celibacy we are called to grow in our capacity for friendships with women and men whose lives touch and enrich ours and who look to us to be sisters to them" (#33).

And the 1982 statement of American Benedictine Women in the Federation of St. Scholastica should be "must" reading in its entirety for American Catholics. Particularly relevant to the present discussion is this paragraph: "Women need to enter into meaningful relationships with both women and men, relationships which are mutually affirming and respectful of the full equality between them." This is a delightful contemporary application of an ideal that reaches back 1,500 years to the very founders of the Benedictine tradition: Benedict and Scholastica.

The need for this dimension of life is recognized even in the cloistered, contemplative groups. In a *New York Times Magazine* article researched for two years by Julia Lieblich and published on July 10, 1983, most of the women she interviewed would agree with the sixty-eight-year-old Maryknoll superior of her cloistered group. Sister Helen Werner noted that life in a cloister does not exclude the possibility of deep platonic relationships with the men and women who visit and with the Sisters in the convent.

This collection of witnesses is a remarkable response to images presented in the soap operas. It is also a testimony that the challenges met by Levinson in his research are being met head on and successfully. The witnesses are also comforting and encouraging to people who share a life-style similar to that of my wife and myself.

We were both married—for the first and still only time—at age thirty-nine. That is rather extraordinary in this culture. All the advice we heard proved that fact. The recommendations made excellent sense for eighteen-year-olds, but were nonsense to thirty-nine-year-olds. So we smiled a lot and listened sympathetically.

After our marriage, we each continued to live our rather independent and responsible lives. I enjoyed singing professionally in the opera: my wife didn't share my enthusiasm. After the final Saturday night performance of each opera, the cast went out for a party. This was usually close to midnight, so the party could last until the early morning.

My wife Jean came to the performance of *Lucia* when Beverly Sills joined the company for that occasion. Jean sometimes came for dress rehearsal, but felt free to skip that if she had other plans. Since she never attended the Saturday night "final" performance of our productions, she never accompanied me to the cast parties. I went alone. But it never failed. Someone would always ask: "Where is your lovely wife this evening?" She is indeed lovely, and I know this was intended to be a compliment and expression of concern for her. But my wife did not attend the performance, and I could see no reason why she should have to stay up until midnight, put on her best clothes, and come downtown just to be with me at the cast party.

Finally, I reached for one of my native New Yorker solutions. The next time someone asked me, "Where's your lovely wife this evening?" I flashed my best "acquired" Midwestern smile and replied: "She's probably home sleeping. After all, we're husband and wife, not Siamese twins." Some Midwesterners would consider that rude and certainly not a joke. Easterners would view it rather differently.

Yet Jean and I respect each other's lives; we cherish each other's personal choices, likes and dislikes, and never impose one upon the other. Indeed, we each retain and cherish our friends of the opposite sex from before we were married. We have always trusted each other, else why would we have married? Besides, marriage is not a condition of slavery, nor does it bestow something like exclusive property rights over one's partner. If marriage is a freely chosen union, it must remain a daily free choice for both partners.

The witness of the life-style of religious women should speak to us in very significant terms. If religious life is somehow something impossible for others to live, then who needs it? If, on the other hand, religious life witnesses to others how life should be lived, how men and women can "break out of rigid categories" and be friends in far more integrated communities than we have known thus far, then it will grow and thrive in the modern Church. Together, all believers will be able to live the gospel as it was intended: for all without distinction.

In 1982, a task force appointed by the archbishop of Milwaukee to study the role of women in the church of southeast Wisconsin wrote a splendid report that included these recommendations: "Because of former religious conditioning, some [women] are slow to realize that claiming one's basic dignity is in harmony with gospel values. Women need to be affirmed and encouraged as they explore nontraditional self-perceptions and roles. . . . even as they insist that their experience be taken seriously, women are insisting that the Church give serious attention to women's experience of God."

It was a hot, Near Eastern midday when Jesus sat down at that well in Samaria. The place was deserted, there was no bucket, his disciples had gone to town to obtain provisions, and Jesus was thirsty. Shortly, a Samaritan woman came by and Jesus struck up a discussion with her.

This story in John's gospel, chapter 4, is not simply recounted but also—like nearly all of John's gospel—very carefully crafted. There are seven exchanges in the story, and the seventh highlights the storyteller's climax.

Jesus opens the dialogue with a request for a drink of water. The woman replies with puzzlement and disdain: "Hey, Jewboy, whom are you asking for water?" It was not only that Samaritans and Jews had no dealings with one another; they also loathed one another. As harsh as the paraphrase sounds, it is likely an accurate rendition of a deliberately insulting retort.

Jesus counters: "You wouldn't be so smart if you knew with whom you were actually dealing. I can give you living water."

The woman is startled because Jesus does not reply with an equally insulting comment, but rather takes the conversation to another plane. Her respect for him increases. "Sir," she addressed him. "What are you talking about? You don't even have a bucket!" Jesus continues: "Anyone who drinks this water will thirst again, but the water I give will quench thirst forever for it will become a fountain within."

The woman replies: "I sure would like that kind of water so that I'd never have to come here again."

Jesus then says: "Call your husband." She says: "I have no husband."

Jesus observes: "You ain't just a-whistlin' 'Dixie,' Lady, you've had five, but who's counting?" The woman replies: "Sir, I see you are a prophet. Let's talk about really important things. Why are we Jews and Samaritans at odds? Where does God really want us to worship him: here in Samaria or in Jerusalem?"

Notice what has occurred. Within the course of five exchanges with Jesus, the woman has moved from "ground zero" in tact and diplomacy, to growing recognition of Jesus' identity. She begins with ethnic identification (Jew), moves to politeness with "sir" (*Kyrios*), and comes to rest — but briefly — upon "prophet," one who speaks the will of God for the here and now.

Jesus answers her question to her great satisfaction, and she then takes still one more step: "Could you be the Messiah?" He replies affirmatively. The evangelist is describing an astonishing growth in faith.

The woman goes off to tell her friends and shares with them her insight into Jesus' identity. They return and ask him to stay with them a while. After listening to him firsthand, they come to believe in him. Their final comment: "No longer does our faith depend on your story. We have heard for ourselves, and we know that this really is the savior of the world."

In John's gospel, this "half-breed" woman is the first one to preach the good news. Her experience of Jesus is quite different from Nicodemus's which has just taken place. She responds to Jesus with on-the-spot insight, and then proceeds to shape her life as preacher immediately. The phrase used in verse 39 to describe what she has related is the same phrase that appears in 17:20 where Jesus prays for the male disciples who will be preaching.

This interpretation has been developed by women biblical scholars who have grounded their conclusions solidly on the evidence of the Greek text. It is an insight that has eluded many readers through centuries, and one can only thank God that increasing numbers of scholars are paying serious attention to women's experience of God, and are reading the sacred texts in a fresh light to help women explore "nontraditional self-perceptions and roles" such as this one highlighted in John's story of the woman at the well.

In his *Cat's Cradle*, Kurt Vonnegut describes God's creation of living creatures out of mud. One of these was man.

"Mud-as-man alone could speak. God leaned close as mud-as-man sat up, looked around and spoke. Man blinked, 'What is the purpose of all this?' he asked politely. 'So, everything must have a purpose?' asked God. 'Certainly,' said the man. 'Then I leave it to you to think of one for all this,' said God. And he went away."

A freely and uniquely shaped wellness spirituality does indeed require a carefully determined personal purpose in life. But as Vonnegut observes, God leaves that entirely in our hands.

THE JOY OF LIVING   ✩ 5

A untie Mame exclaims: "Live! Live! Live! Life is a banquet but most poor suckers are starving to death." Moses made a similar plea to the Israelites: "I set before you today life and death. Choose life!" Jesus too, offered yet another version of the same wish: "I came that you might have life and have it to the full!" All three of these individuals raise the thought that many people are not enjoying life to the full, choosing death, or actually starving at a banquet called "life."

In 1981, the Harvard graduating class of 1956 held its twenty-fifth anniversary reunion. In preparation for the event, a questionnaire was mailed to each member of the class. More than 40 percent of the 664 alumni who responded said that they would not call themselves "contented" or "blessed." The class median annual income that year was $60,000 and the average net worth was $300,000. Moreover, only 59 percent of the respondents would choose the same career today that they did upon graduation. This number was down from the 79 percent who replied affirmatively to the question ten years earlier.

Wellness invites all people to come to the banquet, to take a full and hearty share. But the happiness and fulfillment that is an essential ingredient of a wellness spirituality clearly is not that of laughing all the way to the bank. If life is a bowl of cherries many people wonder why they get only the pits. And if life is a bed of roses, why do the thorns so quickly seem to burst that illusion? No, the authentic, satisfying, fulfilling human joys and pleasures of life that are essential to wellness do not necessarily flow from smooth and untroubled sailing through human existence. As a matter of fact, life's true joys often result from setbacks. The one who has successfully navigated and completed a perfect five-year plan does not seem to be as happy and fullfilled as the one who has had to determine what to do when a gigantic log fell across the plan during the first week of the first month of the first year.

The Joy of Sex?

One night some years ago, the NBC nightly offered a "segment three" that used to feature human-interest items. This particular evening, the commentator focused on a 120-year-old Pakistani who was celebrating his birthday.

That fact alone was not news. Medical science knows that the human body could last for 120 years before any of its parts wear out. The modern problem is not that parts wear out, but rather that they "rust" out. Some parts haven't been used for years, while other parts are routinely "abused."

The real news in this story was the man's claim to have slept with 3,215 women in his lifetime documented with a list of names. While many people would agree that indeed the experience of human sexual intimacy can be one of life's authentic, satisfying, fulfilling, human joys and pleasures, one simply has to wonder about this quantity. Surely, the quality suffered.

Another life-veteran, Joe Bassett, offered a somewhat different perspective. On his 103rd birthday, he was asked for the secret of longevity. He noted that he regularly smoked eight expensive cigars a day, drank wine with every meal plus three or four Scotch and sodas daily, and engaged in other pleasurable pursuits as well. But his real secret was that for one whole year in every ten years, Joe gave up sex. "You know how tired you feel after you've been fooling around?" Joe asked. "That shows it takes a lot out of you. But after a year's rest, you feel like dynamite. You could kill a horse. Best thing in the world for you, and you have nine years to make up for lost time."

Joe reminds me a little of the Bible's reflection on finding true joy and satisfaction in life. Remember Abraham? God made him a mind-boggling, eye-crossing promise: he would father an enormous nation; his progeny would be more numerous than the sands on the seashore. He was seventy-five years old at the time. His wife could not bear children, and eleven years later all Abraham had to show for his efforts was Ishmael, the maid Hagar's child.

But Abraham kept believing, and soon Sarah was ninety years old. One day some visitors came by, and Abraham—both out of loneliness as well as customary Middle Eastern hospitality—implored the visitors to stay a while. Abraham and Sarah wined and dined them superbly well. Afterward, as the men were enjoying fine after-dinner drinks and tobacco, they turned to Abraham and said: "We know how sad you and Sarah are at not being able to have your own children. Well, we predict that next year, when we come by this route again, there will be the pitter-patter of tiny feet in your household."

Sarah was eavesdropping at the tent-flap. When she heard this nonsense, she roared with laughter and all but rolled all over the sand in merriment. "They must be drunk," she said to herself. "Or perhaps they've been sitting in the sun too long."

But the travelers were not amused. And when Sarah tried to pretend she really was not laughing but trying to scratch a hard-to-reach itch, one of the men said: "We're not only predicting the birth of a child, but we predict its sex. It will be a boy. And, Sarah, because you laughed, the child shall be named laughing-boy [Isaac]. Every time you call him you will remember your skeptical laughter, but you will also know the boy brings great pleasure to your life."

Sure enough, everything came to pass as the visitors foretold. And some time later, this same God whom Abraham has been believing and trusting all these many years prompts him to sacrifice his son as a holocaust. (Remember, these were very primitive times.) So Abraham proceeds with the project, only to be stopped by God at the very last minute. "Abe, I like you very much," God said. "You never fail me. My trust in you is well placed. Yes, your progeny will indeed multiply because you have been obedient. Spare your son."

Of the many lessons that have been drawn from this story, the one I offer on this occasion is that when God wants you to enjoy the best life has to offer, he often has you "sacrifice your Isaac." God is not too interested in the ill-fitting, worn-out clothes from one's surplus that are routinely given to "the poor and needy" and then deducted from income taxes. He often asks for the Isaac. The plan that is going so well, the success that seems boundless, and many other similar items are likely candidates.

The Canadian theologian, Penelope Washbourn, phrased it somewhat differently in her book *Becoming Woman*. In the life of every woman, there comes a time of loss. Depending on her age, that loss can be the death of a pet, the loss of a friend who moves to another state, or perhaps the frustration of standing at the altar with bouquet in hand, surrounded by family and friends, only to realize gradually the groom is not going to show up.

A woman can make one of two possible responses: demonic or graceful. In a demonic response, a woman curses all men, swears she will have nothing whatever to do with another man as long as she lives. Effectively she lays down and dies. Although she might live for fifty or seventy more years, she will die a shriveled-up old prune, because she really stopped living at the time of this demonic response to loss.

In a graceful response, a woman will have felt all the same pain and embarrassment. She, too, will want the earth to open and swallow her so as to remove her from the gaze of friends and family. But upon reflection, she will say: "Wow, that was a kick in the head. I'm so ashamed I could die. But that won't solve anything. So, as the poet says, 'I will lay me down and bleed for awhile, then raise me up with a will.' I shan't avoid men in the future, but perhaps I will judge them more carefully. My life will be richer for this experience."

What Washbourn describes is familiar to believers as the "Passover experience" or the "paschal mystery." The basic idea is that one dies to something old to rise to something new. A death and resurrection is essential, and a transformation takes place in the process.

In the days before Vatican II, I used to think I understood this teaching of faith. I believed it could be expressed quite succinctly as: "*After* death, life . . . pleasant, untroubled, forever." So like many other believers, I "offered it up," "stuck it out," "kept the faith," "turned the other cheek," "smiled because God loved me," and performed other similar acts of endurance. Sooner or later it would all be ended, and real life would begin.

Even though convinced this was correct, the outlook was very difficult to live on a daily basis. I began to pray that perhaps God could take me to himself by the time I was thirty-five, because things weren't improving and my strength was sometimes ebbing.

Then at age thirty, a truly providential series of "thunder-bolts in disguise" struck my life. I began the graduate study of scripture and met interesting new people who—in the midst of Vatican II—had a different understanding of the paschal mystery. Soon I realized this new understanding was much better than my old one. The dying-and-rising mystery of faith was not properly interpreted as "*After* death, life," but rather "*Out of* death, life." Seven times seventy-seven times a day a person may have to face some kind of death. The challenge is not simply to endure it and die, but rather to strive to rise again, transformed out of the experience. That is what the paschal mystery means.

Lose Life to Save It

There is yet another way of looking at this notion that one can find true joy and happiness in life by working through and transcending reversals. It is pithily expressed in the gospels in this passage and its parallels: Jesus said to all, "Whoever wishes to be my follower must deny his or her very self, take up the cross each day, and follow in my steps. Whoever would save her life will lose it, and whoever loses her life will save it" (Luke 9:23-24; compare Mark 8:34-35 and Matthew 16:24-25).

The idea of losing life in order to save it already appears five hundred years before Jesus, when Xenophon wrote his *Anabasis* in part to persuade young men to fight old men's wars. He argued that cowards who resisted military service and saved their lives would end up losing reputation, while those who courageously fought and died on the battlefields would perhaps lose life but gain everlasting gratitude and tributes on memorials.

Similar notions are found in Deuteronomy 20:5-9 in the discussion of who should and should not go to war or John 15:13, "Greater love than this no one has, that he lay down his life for his friends." The idea is that one might lose life out of loyalty in friendship or love between two persons, and actually end up gaining a long-lived reputation.

These reflections are variations on a notion that was quite common in the ancient world. The notion was presented in proverb form as "one way of making a whole out of life." The proverb or reflection offers a pattern of living that can be imitated or related on an appropriate occasion.

The gospel passages have a peculiar context: namely, discipleship. One becomes a disciple of Jesus by learning to imitate him, especially in losing life to save it. The immediate impact of this statement is to shatter a normal and widespread understanding: one saves life by saving it, and loses it by being careless or irresponsible. What does Jesus' strange saying mean? It catches the listener up short.

And that is precisely what the saying is intended to do: it reorientates a listener by first disorientating her. It forces a listener to consider the impossible possibility. Chances are, serious attention to such a proverb will have three effects: one's secure vision of life is shattered; God can be known in a moment of discontinuity; a person determines a unique, appropriate and personal answer to the next question: What now?

In Luke's gospel, Jesus says: "Blessed are you when people hate you, and when they ostracize you and insult you and proscribe your name as evil because of the Son of Man. On the day they do so, rejoice and exult, for your reward shall be great in heaven" (6:22). This passage is truly jarring and disturbing. It most certainly shatters the common sense most people make out of life, especially the understanding people have of what it takes to be blessed or truly happy.

It wasn't until after Jesus died and rose again that the disciples began to grasp the idea. During that long hike from Jerusalem to Emmaus, two disciples heard Jesus say: "Thus it is written, that the Christ should suffer and on the third day rise from the dead" (Luke 24:46). When the entire discussion and experience was ended, "the disciples returned to Jerusalem *with great joy*" (24:51).

It was still later in the life of the early Church that the followers of Jesus, after grasping this aspect of the meaning of life, knew what to do next: "When the Sanhedrin called in the Apostles, they beat them and charged them not to speak in the name of Jesus, and let them go. Then they left the presence of the council, rejoicing that they were worthy to suffer dishonor for the *name* . . . and they did not cease teaching and preaching Jesus as Messiah" (Acts 5:40).

Perfect Joy

There is a popular legend in Franciscan lore about Francis of Assisi that expresses this same idea. One day, Francis and Leo were walking from Perugia to the Portiuncula at Assisi. It was winter. Francis said: "Oh Brother Leo, even if Brothers all over the world give outstanding examples of holiness and edification, note well, and write this down: This is not perfect joy."

As they continued, Francis spoke up again: "Oh Brother Leo, if we Brothers could work all kinds of miracles, heal all people, even cause it to rain when needed, note well, and write this down: This is not perfect joy."

Along the way, Francis spoke up three more times in the same way: "Oh Brother Leo, even if we knew all the sacred sciences and could speak in tongues . . . even if we knew everything about the natural world . . . even if we could preach so effectively as to convert all unbelievers, note well, and write this down: This is not perfect joy."

By this time, Brother Leo ran out of patience. "For the love of God, Father Francis, tell me already: what *is* perfect joy?" By the look on Francis's face, Leo could tell that Francis was thinking "What took you so long? I though you'd never ask!"

Then Francis began to describe life's authentic satisfying, fulfilling human joys and pleasure. "Brother Leo, when we arrive at the Friary, frozen to the core, and the Porter refuses us entry and instead chews us out, *and* we endure this patiently knowing he tells it as he sees it, Oh Brother Leo, mark this well: *this* is perfect joy." What a grace, to see ourselves as others see us!

Francis continued: "Of course, we knock again, all the louder. And now the Porter comes out and kicks us around, and we bear this, too. This, Brother Leo, is perfect joy."

For a third time, Francis adds: "And if we plead, but he now physically beats us to within inches of our lives, *yet* we endure all this as our share in the sufferings of Christ — Oh Brother Leo, this is indeed perfect joy."

In his conclusion to this reflection, Francis notes quite simply that perfect joy will result when one realizes the integral part that the paschal mystery, the mystery of dying and rising again, plays in human life. If a reader can separate the true message of Francis from its medieval context, it could probably be recast as follows:

Marvellah Bayh, the late wife of the former Democratic senator from Indiana, Birch Bayh, lived a life typical of many American women in an earlier age. She lived her life "in him, through him, with him, for him." His political career and its success was at the center of her own life. Then, two things happened in her life to change her outlook rather drastically.

When Birch decided to enter the 1971 primaries as a Democratic candidate for president he called a strategy meeting at their home in Indiana but told Marvellah not to come. She was stunned. True, their marriage had its share of ups and downs, but she never expected to be "locked out," as it were, just as he was about to reach for the pinnacle of his career.

Then during a routine physical examination, it was discovered that she had breast cancer, and she underwent a mastectomy. Reflecting later on this experience she wrote: "These years since cancer came to me have been the most rewarding, the most fulfilling, the happiest of my life. I have learned to value life, to cherish it, to put my priorities in order — and to begin my long-postponed dream of being useful in my own right."

Many people who have faced life-threatening situations have found their perspectives on life drastically changed. To a person, many of these people will admit they did not like having cancer, would do anything not ever to get it again, but learned that cancer taught a lesson nothing else did. Life-threatening situations help individuals discover what life is truly all about, what the real joys and satisfactions of life are. Nothing can ever distort that vision again.

After Marvellah's surgery she became quite involved with the American Cancer Society programs and spent the remaining years of her life until her death in 1979 visiting and talking with people all across the country to help them gain the insights and new perspectives she had learned.

Birch's life changed, too. He dropped out of the primary, established an exciting new dimension to his relationship with Marvellah, and worked even harder on equal-rights issues, and especially Title 9, during his remaining time in Congress. Gaining the passage of Title 9 was Birch's tribute to Marvellah from and with whom he learned these precious lessons. Both people lost life, but saved it, and in doing so, found their perfect joy.

Dominican Brother Edward van Merrienboer, Promoter of Justice for the entire Dominican Order in North America, used to be an elementary-school teacher. One day, while waiting to visit with a principal, he decided to slip into first grade and pay a visit to the little people, his favorites. The class was draped in purple, and Brother gasped. "My Lord," he said, "what's all this purple color for? How glum!" It's Lent, Brother," the youngesters told him. "Lint, on my brand new suit?" Then brushing at his sleeves and jacket front he tried to remove this "lint."

"No, Brother," the children shouted even louder to him. "Lent, lent."

"Lent? What does that mean?" asked Brother Ed.

"It's when Jesus died for us, Brother."

"Died for us? For me? I can't believe that. Maybe he died for you, but I'm such a terrible person, Jesus couldn't have died for me" said the Brother.

"Oh yes, Brother, he died for you too" the children insisted.

"I just can't believe that," replied Brother. "You know what might help me believe it? If one of you would die for me, then maybe I could believe that Jesus did. Would one of you die for me?"

The class became dead silent. No one stirred. No one spoke.

They just looked at him. He stood there and waited for some reply. Then he noticed, in the middle of the class, a little tyke who reached his hands out to the far edge of his desk, grabbed the corners, and squeezed until his knuckles began to turn white. At the same time, he gradually raised himself to his full stature as a little person. He said: "Brother, I would die for you . . . but I wouldn't like it!"

CHANGE ☆6

All of life involves change, and if you are not changing then you must be dead. Your obituary will be news to *You*; others have known that you died a long time ago when you stopped changing.

Cardinal Newman expressed the same idea in a slightly different way. "Here below," he wrote, "to live is to change; and to be perfect is to have changed often."

It is perhaps a truism that we simply don't see life at age sixty as we did when we were sixteen. Many of us don't view life the same way at forty as we did when we were thirty-nine. This challenge to change that life directs at us regularly is nothing else but the nagging and repeated call to become one's whole self, to establish, revise, and continue to develop one's wellness, one's personal meaning in life.

Judaism and Christianity have specific names for this challenge to change. The word that occurs most often in the Hebrew scriptures is *šub* (shub), which might be pointedly translated as "getting one's head screwed on straight again."

It is the major element in the preaching of each of the prophets. In the Christian scriptures, the key word is *metanoia*: a transformation of horizons, a broadening of perspectives, a discovery of a totally new range of life-giving and meaning-enriching choices.

The jaded theological jargon word for both of these notions is "conversion." Perhaps the best way to illustrate the meaning of this word is to present two biblical tales from Luke 16. The chapter opens with the story of the rich man and his shrewd steward. The steward wheeled and dealed and perhaps went beyond his own vested interests, or perhaps exposed his master to excessive risks. In any case, when the master learned of this activity, he asked the steward to draw up an account of his stewardship.

The steward summons his debtors and ordered them to change the invoices. Americans often take offense at this "dishonesty." But this is not dishonesty. The steward deprived his master of nothing that was owed to him. What the steward did was to forego his own legitimate commission, which was included in the total sum on the invoices. The master would receive his due. And the steward, shrewd manager that he was, placed these debtors in his debt for a long while. They now "owed" him a favor in return for foregoing his legitimate commission. Jesus praised this business foresight and urged those who seek God's reign to be similarly astute.

A contrast to this story is found in the tale of Lazarus and the rich man. Until their death, there was no indication that anything was awry. If Lazarus was not getting something from the rich man, he was foolish not to go elsewhere to beg. In that culture, it was virtually impossible to ignore giving alms. The compulsion was as strong as the one we might feel about washing our hands after working in the garden and before eating. But the rich man may have been stingy with his alms.

After death, there was a reversal of situations. Lazarus found himself in God's reign, and the rich man was excluded. God also told the rich man it was impossible for him to warn his brothers who still lived.

The stories teach their lessons by contrast. The shrewd steward gave alms in his own way; he shared. The rich man failed to give adequate alms to Lazarus; he did not share. The shrewd steward "wised up before it got too late"; the rich man didn't. The shrewd steward demonstrates conversion; the rich man failed to convert.

Paul, too, "wised up before it got too late" in his life. Most commonly, Christians think that somehow Paul saw the light quite suddenly on the road to Damascus and indeed "wised up." Conversion, however, is much more a process than it is a sudden on-the-spot reversal. Paul was a learned Jew; he had studied at the feet of Gamaliel. He knew Judaism inside and out. He also knew Christianity very well. If his knowledge were only superficial it would not have been worth the effort to persecute Christians as strongly as he did.

But somehow all the pieces did not fit together very well. It was on the road to Damascus that the elusive pieces slipped right into their proper places. This realization or insight, which does indeed come in a flash, was developing in his mind for a long time.

There is another illustration in Paul's life of wising up before it became too late. It can be perceived by reading his letters *not* as they are found in the New Testament (grouped from the longest [Romans] to the shortest [Philemon] but in their approximate chronological sequence.

In the year A.D. 50, or 51, about twenty years after his conversion, Paul sends a letter to his own converts, the Thessalonians, in an effort to encourage them in their faith and offer advice on some of their concerns. One belief widely and commonly held at this time was that Jesus was going to return for the second and final time very soon, perhaps any weekend, to take all his faithful followers with him to eternal bliss.

But people were dying, and the survivors began to worry about them. Would they join Jesus in eternity? Would they have missed out on everything? Paul addresses this concern in 1 Thessalonians 4:13-18. Notice how absolutely convinced he is that *he* (Paul) is not going to die, but will definitely be alive when the Lord returns. Then those who have died Christ will raise up first, and "we" (Paul) the living will "be caught up with them in the clouds to meet the Lord in the air" (4:17).

Contemporary fundamentalists see in this passage the "doctrine" they call "the rapture." Catholics have never had such a doctrine, since they recognize that in this passage Paul is talking primarily about those who have already died. The remainder of the passage is common imagery in the many writings that we possess from this period of time, but which have never been accepted in the Jewish or Christian scriptures.

About five years later, perhaps A.D. 56 or 57, Paul writes two letters to another group of Greek converts, the Corinthians. Paul himself is in Ephesus, has heard of problems in Corinth, and writes a letter to address the problems. As he concludes his first letter, in chapter 15, he discusses the topic of the resurrection of believers; in verse 51 he again voices his firm conviction "not all of us will fall asleep," but all of us will be changed. Paul is still quite certain the Lord is going to return any day soon, and Paul is not going to die at all but be taken by Jesus with him immediately to eternal happiness.

But in his second letter to the Corinthians, written just about two "seasons" later, he refers to an experience in which he was "crushed" to the point of "despairing of life." What happened to shake Paul's conviction?

Acts 19 suggests the answer. It seems that Paul was enjoying good success in his preaching in Ephesus and was winning converts. But workers who made souvenirs to be sold at the temple of the goddess Diana were beginning to suffer a drop in the sales of their wares. So their leader called a meeting (v. 23), explained the problem, and the workers began to rebel.

Indeed, some got hold of Paul's traveling companions, Gaius and Aristarchus, and dragged them into the meeting. Paul himself wanted to attend, but his friends restrained him. Meanwhile, the meeting got out of hand, the group rioted, and the majority did not even know why the gathering was called!

Finally, the town clerk managed to restore order. He advised Demetrius and his workers to take the matter to court, if they liked. With this, the meeting broke up. Paul realized how lucky he was to escape the entire incident unharmed. It finally dawned on him that he very well might not be alive when the Lord returns again in glory. He might die! And from this point on in his epistles, he makes more frequent mention of his mortality. See the references to his own death and resurrection in 2 Corinthians 4:10ff and 11:23ff.

Still later after this letter, perhaps as late as A.D. 62, Paul writes to the Philippians: "I have full confidence that now as always Christ will be exalted through me, whether I live or die" (1:20).

It seems as if Paul had to experience a near catastrophe before he wised up. Recall a similar experience recounted earlier from the life of Marvellah Bayh. It took something as serious as cancer to cause her to reassess her life and redirect it in ways much more to her advantage than before. Similar testimonies from other victims of life-threatening diseases would seem to suggest that indeed one's bottom has to all but fall out before one "wises up." Is this really so?

James Fowler, the researcher who has charted human faith development over a series of stages, identified two stages that are significant for this present question. The third of his six stages, synthetic-conventional faith, is a time of human life when an individual tries to make sense of his life by doing what others do, by conforming, by avoiding "rocking the boat." Such an individual accepts "conventional" behaviors and creates a "synthesis" of the best of these behaviors. Generally, this is how adolescents make decisions. They readily conform to peer pressure. Even while proclaiming freedom and individuality, they tend to dress alike and generally share the same preferences with others in their group. The song alluded to in an earlier chapter best characterizes this stage: "I'll do it the company way, whatever the company says by me is O.K."

From this standpoint of making choices in life, human beings move toward the next stage, which Fowler calls individuative-reflexive (stage four). Here a person takes time to collect opinions, to assess them, and then to select freely the most personally appropriate option. Such an individual is a critical thinker (reflexive) and a free-standing person (individuative). A song that might characterize this stage of making sense out of life might be "I gotta be me," or perhaps even "I did it my way!"

Fowler's research indicates that, ideally, a person develops from stage three (synthetic-conventional) to stage four (individuative-reflexive) in the early or mid-twenties (i.e., usually after high school when a person has begun to establish a more independent position in life).

"For some adults, however," Fowler cautions, "the transition to stage four, if it comes at all, occurs in the thirties and forties. It can be precipitated by changes in primary relation-ships such as divorce, death of a parent or parents, or children growing up and leaving home. Or it can result from the chal-lenges of moving, changing jobs or the experience of the break-down or inadequacy of one's synthetic-conventional faith." (*Stages of Faith Development*, p. 181.) In other words, the bottom indeed has to all but fall out for some people before they wise up!

But for many others, there are countless opportunities for conversion or "wising up" long before a crisis develops. These opportunities are part of the normal process of life; they are occasions for meeting God in such a way that one's life is never quite the same again. The Chicago theologian, Father Edward Braxton, has suggested seven patterns of living in which one can meet God, seven kinds of opportunities in life for wising up. These are the aesthetic pattern of experience, the biolog-ical, social, dramatic, psychological, intellectual, and mystical.

Consider the aesthetic pattern of experience. I used to sing professionally with the Milwaukee Florentine Opera Com-pany Chorus. I well remember the rehearsals for Gounod's *Faust*. Old Dr. Faustus is dejected as the opera opens and wants to end his life when Mephistopheles (the devil) appears to him and offers him youth, a second chance to make sense out of life, in exchange for his soul. Faust agrees.

The devil then fills his life with new happiness. He takes him to a peasant feast, causes him to meet the beautiful Mar-guerite and to become infatuated with her. Then the devil arranges that her brother, Valentin, go off to battle, so that Faust might be free to tryst with her. Marguerite becomes pregnant, and her brother returns. When he discovers this fact, he challenges Faust to a duel. Mephistopheles arranges for Valentin's sword to break, and Faust is able to deal him a mortal blow.

As Valentin lies on the stage in his last moments, the town-folk, having heard the noise of the duel, rush to the scene. Marguerite is the last to arrive. She is horrified that her brother is dying. When he recognizes her, he sings: "Marguerite, *soit maudite!*—May you be cursed!" The peasants gasp and remind him: "Think of yourself, good man. You are dying! Forgive her if you want to be pardoned by God!" But he sings even louder: "May you be cursed, Marguerite. Even if God should forgive you, I do not forgive you. And I die, a brave soldier." With that he falls limp. After a moment of silence, the townsfolk whisper a prayer for him: "May God have mercy on your soul."

I have never been able to rehearse or perform this scene without wanting to kick Valentin squarely in the head. I would want to shake him and yell at him: "My good man, you are dying. Forgive your sister! Don't leave her with this horrid memory, with this heavy load of guilt!" You see, good theater performed well has a way of reaching into one's soul, turning it upside down, and causing changes to take place in the viewer.

I have experienced similar feelings when I played the role of Doc in *West Side Story*. Every night after the performance, I wept over the tragic ending of the story. Why do the teens have to destroy themselves? Why didn't they wise up before it became too late? After the first evening, I felt slightly embarassed. This, after all, was only a play. But it worked its magic each evening. Such cathartic experiences have the power of bringing a participant and a viewer into the presence of God himself, and this encounter prompts the change, the conversion, the readjustment of one's meaning in life.

Or consider the biological pattern of life. Recall the experience I recounted in chapter 3 concerning the unflattering newspaper article about a presentation I had delivered. The message my body sent me then has been repeated on similar occasions since that time. A few years ago I was invited by the Archdiocese of Milwaukee to deliver a major address at its annual religious congress. I was honored and excited. The invitation arrived in December, and I had my presentation completely prepared by the end of February. I polished it in succeeding months as I awaited the set date in August.

About three weeks before the congress, I felt a pain in my tooth and suspected an impacted wisdom was preparing to act up. The pain increased, so I called my dentist. He was on vacation, but his assistants advised me — as I had expected — to take aspirin for the pain and make an appointment for surgery after the congress. Much to my surprise, the pain subsided and disappeared one week before the congress and never returned.

When I showed up at the dentist's office in September, he took new x-rays and then returned to discuss the results. He asked if I had been under stress in the last month or two. I told him about the major address at the congress and said that I am always under stress on such occasions, just as actors and singers become stressed before a concert or performance. He understood this well. He, too, used to sing in the opera chorus.

He then explained that there was no reason why my tooth should have been bothering me. There was no decay, no pressure on nerves, nothing to indicate that it could cause pain. If I insisted, he'd schedule surgery, but he advised against it. I laughed and declined the surgery. I should have guessed! Once again my body was sending a message.

I was concerned about my address. Though it was well prepared months in advance, I allowed my concern for the best possible presentation in this diocese where I had been living for more than ten years to get the better of me. I was spending entirely too much time worrying about it. So my body gave me something else to worry about, to distract my attention. And it succeeded! The tolerable mild pain was presistent enough to distract my attention from the address. By the time my appointed turn came up in the program, I was relaxed, quite at ease and eager to begin. The address went as well as any of my presentations. There should never have been any cause for concern. I can only think of the psalmist: "I give you thanks, O Lord, that I am fearfully, wonderfully made; wonderful are your works!"

As I have continued to learn more and more about the human body — *my* body — I have to marvel at the brilliant God who created this magnificent handiwork. By not thwarting the body's communication system with chemicals of one or another kind, a person actually possesses a magnificent guide to good living, a sure path back to the Creator who doesn't always use burning bushes or dreams and visions as her media.

Finally, consider the dramatic pattern of human life. Even the most drab existence has a dramatic dimension. One needs to learn how to reflect and identify these experiences. In 1970, I was completing the course work for my doctorate in scripture and according to the procedures had determined to write my qualifying exams that spring. I went to the department of theology on a Monday morning to pick up the questions and brought back my completed exam on Wednesday.

I felt quite good about the experience. I had managed to focus all of the queston on the baptism of Jesus, a topic that I knew exceptionally well, since I had planned to write my dissertation on that topic. On Friday of that same week, I was to make an oral defense of my exam with the five assigned examiners.

Four of these examiners were biblical scholars who went over the exam in great detail. It was an exhausting experience, and as I turned to face the last examiner I felt I could now relax. He was not a biblical scholar, but rather a Luther specialist. The rules required that one of the examiners be a specialist in a different but related field of theology. Further, he was out of town all week doing research in Chicago and had returned only that very day. He could not have had very much time to spend reviewing my exam. And finally, he was and is a very good friend, an easygoing sort of person who could be gentle even while demanding.

His first question to me was: "Who the hell cares about the baptism of Jesus?" I was immediately paralyzed. What did he mean? Why did he say this? As I slowly withdrew the arrow from my forehead, I tried to formulate a response. Sensing my confusion, he went on to explain that the exam was good, and that my performance in both the written and oral segments was quite acceptable. But if all I would do upon completing my degree was to delve deeply into detail and dwell on the heights of an academic Mount Olympus, what good would that be? Who would know or care?

Well of course I could develop the practical relevance of this entire enterprise, but I was rather unprepared at the moment because of the nature of this exam. At any rate, he concluded his discussion, the exam ended, and I was promoted to candidacy by a unanimous vote of the committee.

I slept well that night and decided to take the next day, Saturday, off from my studies. I wouldn't go to the library but would just enjoy the warm and sunny day that had dawned in Milwaukee. After breakfast, I walked down Wisconsin Avenue to Lake Michigan and then headed back to my apartment. As I returned through the heart of downtown, I came upon a parade heading toward the lakefront. This was Armed Forces Day, and the military were marching together with other bands and groups. I like parades and paused — on the sunny side of the street — to watch.

This was the Vietnam era, and the Armed Forces Day parade was not popular with all citizens. On my side of the street, there was a group of young people — perhaps students — who occasionally shouted out "Peace now!" as they flashed the "V" sign toward the marchers, especially the military groups. Across the street were some stalwart citizens who shouted back at the youths: "Aw shut up, you hippies! Go home! Get outta here!" This went on for about an hour or so, and I stood there amused by the peaceful exchanges between these two groups. It made me think of my home city, Brooklyn, New York, where this kind of exchange on any topic is rather common.

Soon a police officer came along and stood next to me, and I was feeling even more comfortable. This was America, a free country, where a parade can take place in support of one ideal, and spectators were free to voice their opinions on the sidelines supporting other ideas. How beautiful!

The next time that the young people ran toward the curb to flash the peace sign at the marchers, the officer took his walkie-talkie, spoke into it, and within three minutes a paddy wagon came down the street near the curb from the direction opposite the parade route. It stopped right by us, the doors flew open, officers jumped out, grabbed the protestors, threw them into the wagon, shut the doors, and the wagon departed.

As I stood there watching — paralyzed once again — I could hear the sentence from last evening in my ears: "Who really cares about the baptism of Jesus?" I was ashamed of myself for just standing there. And the next morning when I read the newspaper account of the parade, the article reported: "Yesterday's Armed Forces parade was a successful event. It took place without incident or arrest." And I wept as I remembered the lines again: "Who really cares about the Baptism of Jesus? . . . What good is your 'theology' if it doesn't touch the daily lives of ordinary folk, if it can't address what you witnessed and experienced?"

Though I have shared this anecdote with the examiner in question, he has no recollection of his specific statements. He remembers with pleasure the success of the exam but nothing more. For me, the events of that week constituted an encounter with the God I study about, talk about, and write about. That encounter altered the way I "do theology" and changed the place where I do it.

Father Braxton observes that the seven areas or patterns of experience he has listed occasionally — as in my examples — cause things, persons, or events that were hitherto unnoticed to become very vivid, present, and influential. Issues that until this moment were previously of no concern now become of utmost importance. And gradually, in and through these experiences, a person learns to see God and experience her as the radical source of meaning in life.

These experiences help bring about change. This encounter with God causes a person to review, to revalue and to reconstruct personal faith. The hope is to wise up before it becomes too late, and the process involves building up a meaning for life, revising it, building it again, revising it again, and on and on in this never-ending process of conversion.

A disciple of Thomas Merton observed that Merton believed eternal bliss could not be an ecstatic high that one gained in one moment upon entering heaven and which remained at that level for ever. Merton said there would have to be an "off" button to press when one needed a rest.

Another perspective might point to the "process of human existence" both here below as well as after death and resurrection. As the process doesn't seem to be completed here, it would seem fitting that the process continue even then. To become static and "finished, complete, perfect" forever seems unbefitting of God and of eternity. This is why wellness can be defined as "a never-ending, ever-expanding experience of pleasurable and purposeful living shaped by the free choice of life-sustaining and life-enriching options that are deeply rooted in spiritual values and religious beliefs."

In American culture, we seem to have a difficult time with forgiveness. The renewed effort to reinstate the death penalty is only the most recent illustration of a pattern. Political analysts suggest that President Ford's pardon of President Nixon was at least partially responsible for Ford's failure to win election to the presidency. Gubernatorial pardons are granted but rarely announced on the front pages. One will regularly find them in the fine print of the classified section of the newspapers.

I remember the case of John Gacy in Chicago. This man was accused and then found guilty of murdering some thirty young men and burying them under his home. The jury deliberated the case in March 1980, and found Gacy guilty of the crimes as charged. When the jury returned again with the verdict that he should die in the electric chair, this decision drew a burst of applause and cheers in the courtroom from friends and relatives of the victims.

When I heard about this reaction, I felt sick. Then I reflected that if my son, or my brother, or close friend were one of those victims, perhaps I would have joined in the cheers and applause. But I think I would have later felt embarrassed.

Later that week, my wife Jean and I were leading a group celebration of a Passover Seder. This traditional meal is preceded by a recounting of the story of the Exodus, the liberation of the Jews from oppression in Egypt thousands of years ago. As the story comes upon the ten plagues, the leader offers advice from the Talmud:

"Our Rabbis taught: when the Egyptian armies were drowning in the sea, the Heavenly Hosts broke out in songs of jubilation. God silenced them and said: 'My creatures are perishing, and you sing songs of praise?'" (Sanhedrin B, 39b).

Holy Week coincided with the Passover season that year, and Christians recalled that from his cross Jesus prayed: "Father, forgive them, for they know not what they do!"

Still, the response to the Gacy verdict reminds us all that the process of wising up is practically never ending. Rose Bird, the Chief Justice of the California Supreme Court, sometimes reflects on the positive effects of her bout with breast cancer. She notes that death has a forceful way of teaching what life is all about. Like many other cancer victims, she too is grateful that she had the experience, though she would do all in her power to avoid it.

The specific lessons she learned from her experience concerned herself and others. She learned what she really wanted out of life, how precious life is, and how very special people and friends are. "It is our relationship with others," she noted, "especially those we love, that give the fullest meaning to life. I don't think I ever really knew that, emotionally or intellectually, until my second bout with cancer."

A second bout with cancer! Chief Justice Bird demonstrates that it is never too late to learn. It is always possible to wise up before it is too late. The opportunities are available in the ordinary experiences of day-to-day living.

CONCLUSION ✸

A mericans are obsessed with "do-it-yourself" programs. This is a natural corollary to their emphasis
upon personal freedom. Some years ago, an enterprising
group of people decided to design and produce a teach-
yourself-how-to-ski program. They obtained experts in
curriculum design who composed a superb didactic package.
Then they realized that this teach-yourself-program could be
greatly enhanced if it were accompanied by films illustrating
the correct principles of skiing.

They sent a camera crew to Europe to film Jean-Claude
Killey as he skied his favorite slopes. When they returned to
America and developed the films, they were aghast to discover that Killey illustrated none of the principles in the program! Indeed, he contradicted many of them, and yet he
remains a champion skier.

Then it dawned on the enterpreneurs: they had discovered
"holistic skiing"! At first, I laughed in cynical scepticism.
Anything to make a buck. But quickly I realized they were

right. It is not enough to know some abstract principles— even if these notions were deduced from the actual practices of many expert skiers and other specialists. It is rather equally, if not more, important to know how "my" body feels on "these" skis in "these" bindings on "this" day. It is important to know how to experience and respond to these snow conditions and air currents. A skier who can keep all these things not only in mind but also in her entire being is truly skiing holistically. The end result, the performance, turns out to be far greater and much more complex than the sum of all the ingredients.

Wellness is a holistic spirituality in the very same way. It is a highly personal way of making sense out of life. Someone who is sightless or a quadriplegic is quite capable of being well in spite of a reduced capacity for physical exercise. A diabetic can also be well despite dietary restrictions. There is no infallible list of absolutely essential ingredients for the holistic spirituality, wellness.

The key element in this concept is free choice, and it can be exercised around basic life concerns like meaning, satisfaction, values and self-esteem. Freedom involves an ability to change, to change often. This frequent change should, of course, be for the better, though that is not necessarily always the case. Still, it is never too late to wise up, to "convert," to find finally the Hound of Heaven.

SUGGESTED READING   ⊰⊱

Introduction

Carmody, John. *Holistic Spirituality*. Ramsey, N. J.: Paulist Press, 1983.

Hays, Edward M. *The Ethiopian Tatoo Shop*. (Rt. 1, Box 247) Easton, Kans. (66020) Forest of Peace Books, 1983.

Pilch, John J. *St. Francis: Model of Wholeness*. Kansas City, Mo.: NCR Cassettes, 1982.

_____. *Wellness: Your Invitation to Full Life*. Minneapolis: Winston Press, 1981.

_____. *Wellness: A Holistic Spirituality*. (P.O. Box 11724) Pittsburgh (15228): Thesis Theological Cassettes,

Chapter 1 / You Alone Do It

Arnold, John D., and Bert Tomkins. *How to Make the Right Decisions*. (1000 East Huron St.) Milford, Minn. (48042): Mott Media, 1982.

Chapter 2 / But You Don't Do It Alone

Johnson, Luke T. *Decision Making in the Church: A Biblical Model.* Philadelphia: Fortress Press, 1983.

Malina, Bruce J. *The New Testament World: Insights from Cultural Anthropology.* Atlanta: John Knox Press, 1981.

Chapter 3 / Motivation: Self-esteem and Clear Values

Bruhn, John G., and Steward Wolf. *The Roseto Story.* Norman, Okla.: University of Oklahoma Press, 1979.

Schuller, Robert H. *Self-esteem: The New Reformation.* Waco, Tex.: Word Books, 1982.

Vargiu, James, and Naomi Remen. "What is Health For? Human Priorities in Health Care." *Western Journal of Medicine* 131 (December 1979): 471-72.

Chapter 4 / Purpose in Life

Moran, Gabriel. "Work, Leisure, and Religious Education." *Religious Education* 74 (March/April 1979): 159-70.

"Task Force Report on the Role of Women in the Church of Southeast Wisconsin." Milwaukee: Archdiocese of Milwaukee, 1982.

Chapter 5 / The Joy of Living

Beardslee, William A. "Saving One's Life by Losing It." *Journal of the American Academy of Religion* 47 (March 1979): 59-72.

Chapter 6 / Change

Braxton, Edward. "The New Rite of Reconciliation in American Culture." *Chicago Studies* 15 (1976): 185-98.

Fowler, James W. *Stages of Faith.* San Francisco: Harper & Row, 1981.